CAN I WILL I COOK! COOK!

Everyday Cooking for Everyday People

CONTENTS

MAIN COURSES

DESSERTS

SANDWICHES

PASTES, SAUCES + DRESSINGS

Introduction

This book reflects a desire to instil healthier eating habits into all communities. For many years now, a strategy of both Government and the media has been to instruct us all about the benefits of eating healthy foods and how choosing those foods will prolong our health and improve our overall wellbeing.

Clearly, eating well and enjoying yourself whilst doing so will have some of those benefits, but for many people whose lives are busy managing an everyday struggle, due maybe to the pressures of running a family or making ends meet, the practice of eating healthily and enjoying the pleasure of preparing food to sit and enjoy is that much harder.

Can Cook Will Cook acknowledges these difficulties but sets out to show that whatever your circumstances and however busy you are, you can always find something interesting to cook and the time to cook and enjoy the food you have cooked. Furthermore, with a bit of commitment and routine, you will realise that wanting to cook and to share the cooking experience can become a really exciting part of your day – everyday.

We hope you enjoy using the book, preparing these simple recipes, experimenting with food and sharing your cooking experience with your family and friends. There is something in here for everyone.

About Sure Start and Fresh Cafés

Sure Start is all about giving children and parents the best chance to strongly live and thrive as a family and as individuals. Our Sure Start has been around since 2000 and has done some amazing work with hundreds of families who otherwise would have had little or no support. Every year we look for new ways to work with people and improve the chances of children. This year we decided (amongst everything else that goes on) to 'play' with food and all the great things you can do with it.

To get started we used our cafés as a base we now have 3 cafés trading under the brand "Fresh". Through Fresh, we have started to get a small number of people, either as customers or as our trainees, to think about their diet and view cooking and eating as fun. Then as a consequence of all this activity, we have been going along creating a neat little business.

Now we want to spread our methods to a wider and much larger audience. The creation of this book, which, together with the ideas we have to expand our services, will in the coming years hopefully see us grow into a vibrant and commercially strong social enterprise, creating lots of opportunity and jobs along the way.

For more information visit www.surestartspeke.org

The Can Cook Initiative

If you can cook, are comfortable cooking and cook regularly and confidently, this book is not really for you – although we bet you find something in here that you will want to try. However, if you think you can't cook (and everybody can) and so won't cook (or rarely feel the urge to) this book is very much for you. It is packed with easy recipes and made up of really tasty foods available from every supermarket.

At our community cafés, we have always experimented by introducing new foods into our menu and tempting our customers away from the bad habits and convenience that make meal times something of a chore rather than being one of the most important parts of the day. For us, we want to encourage people to sit down, relax, taste, discuss their food and then later, to go home and prepare the same types of food for their families.

Can Cook Will Cook was originally a short training course to introduce basic cookery techniques to people who hardly ever cooked and who viewed the need for such things as herbs and spices in cooking as something quite alien, even 'weird'. The training was a great success and it inspired us to want to share some of the recipes we and our trainees have used with you.

Our slogan is "Everyday Cooking for Everyday People" and our passion is about just that – getting everyone to enjoy food, every single day. We have a great time managing our cafés, teaching people the basics of cookery and creating new ways to share this experience with anyone who is starting to cook and / or looking for recipes that are fun and easy to prepare.

This is not a celebrity chef book with lots of researchers and a big budget to make it all incredibly slick. This is a book about us all mucking in to get it done and real grass roots cookery. If we can get you to take time to play with our recipes – and as you become more confident swop and change the ingredients to create versions you can call your own – Can Cook Will Cook will have achieved much of what it set out to do.

Please read it, use it, get it messy and let us know all about it.

robbie.davison@surestartspeke.org

Tony and the Trainees

3 years ago Tony became our chef. He joined us saying "I want a new challenge, to cook and do something different far away from restaurants". Slowly but surely, and with many successes along the way, he and his café colleagues (Angie, Margie and Di) started to change the way food is served at our centre. With a new type of community café in place, he and the team – ready for another challenge – jumped right into teaching parents how to cook.

The faces you see throughout this book are of Tony, the parents (and sometimes grandparents) and their children who have either taken part in our training or who came along to one of our 'foodie' events.

The pictures tell their own stories...

Things you might need

All the ingredients in our recipes are available from supermarkets. We hope you are lucky enough to have a specialist deli or good butcher or fishmonger nearby to enable you to 'keep it local' but in the real world we know for most people this is not always an option, so supermarkets it is.

That said, you will need a few utensils – we are not saying go out and buy everything at once, just pick bits up as you need them. We have provided a guide price for you to purchase items that will do the job.

Two sharp knives, one 8 inch, one 4 inch = £12 for the two
Two plastic chopping boards, one for meat, one for veg = £5
A pestle and mortar to crush up your spices = £5 – £8
A hand blender for your soups= £10 – £20
A measuring jug = £1
A couple of wooden spoons = £2
A colander = £2
A large plastic mixing bowl for all those salads and desserts = £3
Scales = £5
A potato ricer for the smoothest mash ever (Ikea have good ones) = £5
A garlic press, for times when you don't want to chop = £3
Ramekin dishes for starters or serving and baking little puds = 5 for £10

How much?

Alongside each recipe we have calculated an approximate cost to help you budget for each meal. Each price assumes you have a stock of items such as herbs, spices and oils.

5-a-day

Eating five portions of fruit and vegetables every day is the simplest way for your body to get the vitamins, minerals and other nutrients it needs. You can start by including two portions with each of your meals.

Easy ways to get 5-a-day

Add fruit and veg to your favourite recipes – such as peppers and sweetcorn to pasta sauces and pizza toppings, peas and beans to soups, root veg to mashed potato.

Snack on fresh and dried fruit. Fruit is less fattening than most processed snacks, and a healthy alternative for mid-morning or mid-afternoon.

Have a fruity pudding or add fruit to your breakfast. Don't stop at strawberry yogurts – try adding banana or fresh blueberries to your cereal or raisins to your porridge.

Use frozen veg if it's easier. It counts.

Eat more beans and pulses. Adding them to salads is easy and canned butter or kidney beans are quick to prepare – just make sure they're low in salt.

Make a smoothie for breakfast by blending your favourite fruits together.

What counts as one of my five a day?

All fruit and vegetables count: fresh, frozen, canned or dried; with the following exceptions:

Pure fruit juices and fruit smoothies only count as one portion per day, no matter how much you drink.
Beans and pulses can only count as one portion per day.
Potatoes don't count at all.

What's a 5-a-day portion?

As a general rule, a portion is 80g of fruit and veg which is roughly a handful. The following all count as 1 portion:

1 apple, banana, pear, orange
2 plums, satsumas, kiwi fruit
half a grapefruit or avocado
1 large slice of melon or pineapple
3 heaped tablespoons of veg, beans and pulses, or fruit salad
1 heaped tablespoon of raisins or sultanas
3 dried apricots
1 cupful of grapes, cherries or berries
1 dessert bowlful of salad
1 small glass (150ml) of pure fruit juice

How to get the most nutrition from fruit and veg

Preparing fruit and veg can cause some of the vitamins and minerals to be lost. Here's how to keep hold of them:

Eat fresh fruit and veg as soon as possible.
Don't overcook; crunchy is healthy.
Cook in as little water as possible or steam.
Don't leave cut veg open to air, light or heat.
Don't keep food hot for too long.

SOUPS

We love soups, everybody loves soups.
They're so quick and easy and last for days.
Try these out to get you started.

Celeriac and Potato Soup

Fry off the onion and garlic in the butter and olive oil on a low heat until soft, taking care not to colour the garlic (this should take about 5 minutes).

Add the thyme leaves, potatoes, celeriac and stock and bring to the boil, then simmer for about 40 minutes until the vegetables are tender.

Add the cream then bring back to the boil and purée the mixture with a hand blender until smooth and silky. Season according to your taste with salt and pepper.

Pour into 4 soup bowls and garnish with some flat leaf parsley and finely sliced celery.

INGREDIENTS
2 white onions diced
4 cloves of garlic chopped
2 knobs of butter
A splash of olive oil
2 tbls of thyme leaves
400g of celeriac cubed
400g of potatoes cubed
2 pints of vegetable stock
100ml of double cream
Salt and pepper

Serves 4

£3.50

Leek and Potato Soup

Fry the onion and garlic in the butter and olive oil on a low heat until soft but not coloured (this should take about 5 minutes).

Add the potatoes, leeks and stock, bring to the boil then simmer for about 30 minutes until the vegetables are tender.

Add the cream and mustard then bring back to the boil and purée the mixture with a hand blender until smooth and silky. Season according to your taste.

Pour into soup bowls and garnish with quickly fried shredded leeks.

Serve with warm crusty bread.

INGREDIENTS
2 onions diced
2 cloves of garlic chopped
2 knobs of butter
A splash of olive oil
600g of leeks
1 tbls of Dijon mustard
300g of potatoes cubed
2 ½ pints of vegetable stock
100ml of double cream
Salt and pepper

Serves 4

 £4.00

Rich Roast Tomato and Basil Soup

Pre-heat the oven to gas mark 6. Slice the tomatoes in half and place into an oven proof dish, then peel and slice the onions and garlic and add to the same dish. Sprinkle over the balsamic vinegar, olive oil and sugar, then mix and bake in the oven for about 1 hour, stirring from time to time until they have softened and coloured.

Transfer to a large saucepan, add the stock and simmer over a medium heat for about 25 – 30 minutes or until the vegetables start to disintegrate. Stir in the basil and liquidise.

Finally, pass the soup through a sieve and season according to your taste.

Serve with warm bread.

INGREDIENTS
1.5kg of tomatoes
4 large red onions
4 tbls of balsamic vinegar
2 tsp of caster sugar
4 tbls of olive oil
3 pints of vegetable stock
2 large handfuls of fresh basil
2 cloves of garlic
Salt and pepper

Serves 4

£4.00

Mushroom and Tarragon Soup

In a large saucepan heat the olive oil and butter, then add the onions and garlic and cook on a low to medium heat for about 10 minutes.

Add the mushrooms, lemon juice and stock and simmer for about 20 – 25 minutes.

Take the pan off the heat and stir through the cream and tarragon, then liquidise until smooth.

Season and serve with warm crusty bread.

INGREDIENTS
400g of button mushrooms
350g of chestnut mushrooms
1 onion sliced
2 cloves of garlic chopped
Juice from $1/2$ a lemon
$1^{1}/_{2}$ pints of vegetable stock
250ml of double cream
4 tbls of chopped fresh tarragon
Salt and pepper
1 tbls of olive oil
50g of butter
Crusty bread (organic is best)

Serves 4

£4.00

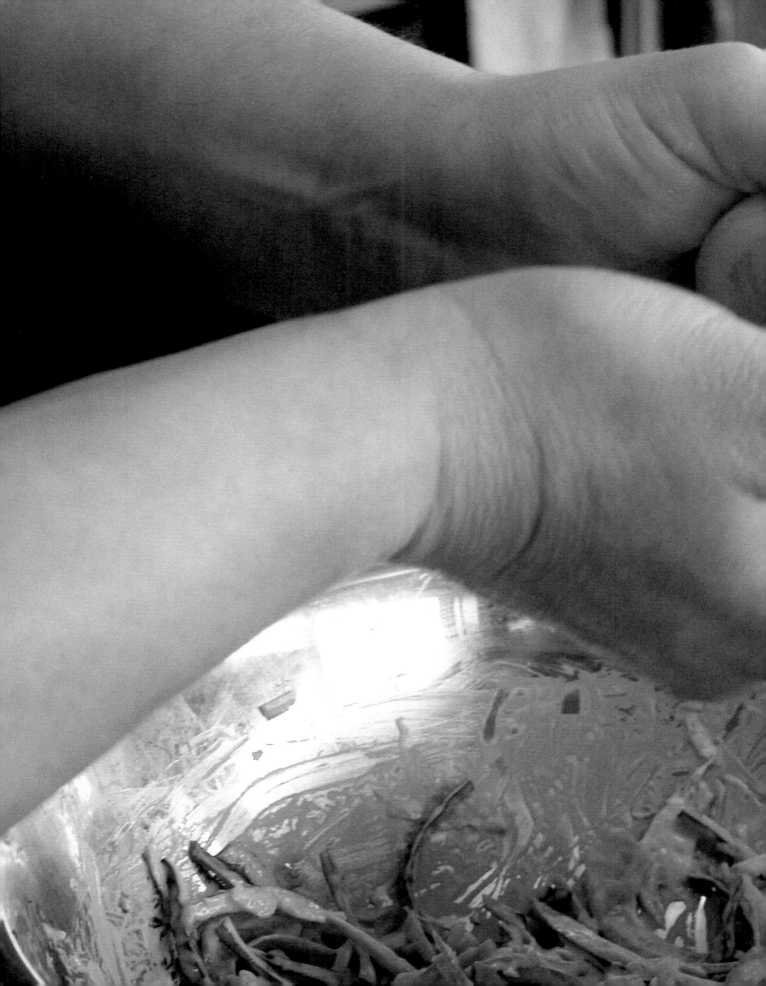

SALADS

All fresh and full of the taste of summer
with a bit of a twist.

Tomato and Mozzarella Salad

Slice each tomato into quarters, peel and finely slice the red onion, then place in a bowl.

Tear the basil leaves into the bowl and add the olive oil, $1/2$ a teaspoon of black pepper and $1^1/_2$ teaspoons of sea salt and mix well.

Take the mozzarella out of its packet and drain off the liquid, then tear it into bite size pieces and stir through the salad. Serve.

Note: When buying the mozzarella you want the type that comes as a soft ball with liquid in a bag or pot, not the hard type used for pizza. Maldon sea salt is a flaky salt with a distinctive taste and works really well with this dish and indeed any other, it is however slightly more expensive. If you don't have Maldon, ordinary salt will do but its not as good.

INGREDIENTS

6 ripe tomatoes
$1/2$ a red onion
2 whole mozzarella
10 large fresh basil leaves
3 tbls of olive oil
Maldon sea salt
Black pepper

Serves 4

£3.50

Rice Salad

Cook the rice according to the instructions on the packet. Once cooked, put the pan into the sink under running cold water to chill, drain well and place the rice into a bowl.

De-seed and dice the peppers and tomatoes, add to the rice. Then peel and dice the onion, chop the celery and add to the rice. De-seed and finely dice the chilli, chop the herbs, then stir into the salad along with the lemon juice and olive oil.

Season according to your taste and serve.

INGREDIENTS

1 cup of long grain rice
1 red pepper
1 green pepper
4 tomatoes
1 red onion
2 sticks of celery
1 red chilli
2 tbls of fresh parsley
2 tbls of fresh mint
2 tbls of olive oil
Juice from 1 lemon
Salt and pepper

Serves 4

£3.50

Roasted Vegetable Salad

Peel and de-seed the butternut squash, slice in half lengthways then slice across the lengths making pieces about 1cm thick and place into an oven proof dish. Next, top and tail the courgette, then slice in half lengthways, and again slice across at about 1cm thick and add to the squash.

De-seed and cube the red pepper and cut the mushrooms into quarters, add both to the pan, then peel and thickly slice the red onion adding to the pan. Next, add the garlic, olive oil and cumin to the vegetables and, using your hands, rub into the vegetables. Add a good pinch of salt and pepper.

Bake the vegetables in a preheated oven at gas mark 6 for 25 – 30 minutes, checking and stirring regularly. The time the vegetables take to cook will vary depending on size but they are ready when they are all quite tender and slightly golden. When they are cooked, remove from the oven, stir through the rocket, and serve immediately with the grated parmesan sprinkled on top.

INGREDIENTS

½ butternut squash
1 courgette
1 red pepper
1 red onion
5 cup mushrooms
1 handful of rocket salad
1 clove of crushed garlic
2 tsp of ground cumin
4 tbls of olive oil
Salt and pepper
3 tbls of grated, fresh parmesan

Serves 4

£4.00

Roasted Vegetable and Couscous

To cook the couscous, place into a bowl and pour enough boiling water over to only just cover, stir well and cover with cling film for 10 minutes.

De-seed and chop the peppers, peel and chop the onion, chop the mushrooms and leek and place all the vegetables into a baking tray along with the thyme and crushed garlic. Sprinkle with olive oil and a little salt and pepper, mix well and bake in a pre-heated oven, gas mark 7 for about 25 minutes, stirring from time to time.

Remove the cling film from the bowl with the couscous and run a fork through it to help it separate. Add the juice from the orange, chop the dill and stir through the couscous.

Finally, add the roasted vegetables and stir well using a tablespoon, season according to your taste and serve hot or cold.

INGREDIENTS

2 cups of couscous
1 red pepper
1 yellow pepper
1 red onion
5 mushrooms
1 leek
1 clove of garlic
3 sprigs of thyme
3 tbls of olive oil
Salt and pepper
3 tbls of fresh dill
Juice from 1 orange

Serves 4

£3.50

Greek Salad

Take off the outer leaves of the lettuce and discard. Wash and dry the inner leaves and place into a bowl.

De-seed and dice the pepper, halve the tomatoes and peel and dice the red onion before adding to the lettuce.

Peel, core and dice the cucumber, slice the olives and add both to the salad.

Mix the olive oil, lemon juice and oregano together and mix into the salad.

Break up the feta cheese and mix carefully into the salad, season with black pepper and serve.

INGREDIENTS

1 little gem lettuce
1 yellow pepper
10 cherry tomatoes
½ a cucumber
½ a red onion
10 pitted black olives
50g of feta cheese
3 tbls of olive oil
Juice from 1 lemon
2 tsp of dried oregano
Black pepper

Serves 4

£3.50

Mixed Bean Salad

Wash and drain the beans and chickpeas and place into a bowl.

Peel and finely dice the red onion, cut the tomatoes into quarters and add to the beans.

Mix the olive oil, balsamic vinegar and finely sliced garlic together and mix into the salad.

Finally, roughly chop the herbs and stir into the salad. Season according to your taste and serve.

INGREDIENTS

200g of red kidney beans
200g of chickpeas
200g of butter beans
200g of borlotti beans
1 red onion
10 cherry tomatoes
½ a clove of garlic
2 tbls of balsamic vinegar
4 tbls of olive oil
2 tbls of fresh dill
2 tbls of fresh coriander
Salt and pepper

Serves 4

£3.50

Salmon Pasta Salad – serves four as a lunch

Bring a large pan of salted water to a rapid boil and cook the pasta according to the instructions on the packet. When cooked, place the pan into the sink under cold running water for about 3 – 5 minutes to cool the pasta down and stop it from cooking any more. Drain and set aside.

While the pasta is cooking cut the salmon into strips and then into about 1cm cubes, place into a bowl along with the olive oil and smoked paprika, mix well and leave for about 10 minutes to marinade.

De-seed and finely slice the peppers, peel and finely slice the red onion and place both into a clean bowl along with the pasta. Heat a frying pan and add all the salmon and olive oil mixture, cook for about 3 minutes on a high heat, then pour all of the salmon and oil into the pasta. Add the lemon zest and juice and the dill, then mix well and season to taste.

INGREDIENTS

300g penne pasta
170g fillet of salmon
1 red pepper
1 yellow pepper
1 red onion
3 tbls of olive oil
1 tsp of smoked paprika
Juice and zest from 1 lemon
2 tbls of chopped fresh dill
Salt and pepper

£4.00

Cucumber and Mint Salad

Cut the cucumber in half lengthways and using a teaspoon scrape out the seeds from the middle.

Cut the cucumber at a slight angle in $\frac{1}{2}$ cm thick slices and place into a bowl, then peel and very finely slice the onion, adding it to the cucumber.

Shred the mint leaves and add to the salad along with the yoghurt and lemon juice, stir and let stand for a couple of minutes. Season according to your taste and serve.

INGREDIENTS

1 cucumber
1 white onion
3 tbls of mint leaves
4 tbls of Greek yoghurt
Juice from $\frac{1}{2}$ a lemon
Salt and pepper

 ₴2.00

Tuna Pasta Salad – serves four as a lunch

Bring a large pan of salted water to a rapid boil and cook the pasta according to the instructions on the packet. When cooked, place the pan into the sink under cold running water for about 5 minutes to cool the pasta down and stop it from cooking any more. Drain and set aside.

While the pasta is cooking, open the tuna and drain off the brine, squeezing out as much as you can, then place into a bowl along with the drained pasta.

Peel and finely dice the red onion then de-seed and finely dice the peppers adding to the pasta. Add the juice from the lemon and the mayonnaise then mix well. Stir through the tarragon and season according to your taste. Serve with a handful of mixed leaves.

INGREDIENTS

300g penne pasta
2 small cans of tuna
1 red onion
1 green pepper
1 red pepper
Juice from 1 lemon
6 tbls of mayonnaise
2 tbls of chopped fresh tarragon
Salt and pepper
4 good handfuls of mixed leaves

₴2.50

POTATOES + VEG

No meat or fish, just simple dishes that concentrate on spreading the word about the versatility of potatoes and veg.

Creamy Garlic Potatoes

Place the potatoes into a pan of cold water and bring to the boil, turn down the heat and simmer for about 20 – 25 minutes until only just cooked. Take off the heat and drain until slightly cooled, then cut the potatoes in half lengthways and place into an oven proof dish.

In a bowl, mix the wine, cream and garlic together, add a good pinch of salt and pepper and pour over all of the potatoes, lightly stir in the thyme and give it a little shake.

Bake the potatoes in a pre-heated oven on gas mark 7 for about 10 – 15 minutes.

INGREDIENTS

600g of new potatoes
300ml of double cream
100ml of white wine
2 cloves of crushed garlic
3 sprigs of thyme
Salt and pepper

Serves 4

£2.20

(if you already have wine in the house)

Herby Potatoes

Place the potatoes in their skins into a pan of cold water and bring to the boil, then turn down the heat and simmer for about 20–25 minutes until only just cooked. When cooked, drain and leave to cool slightly, peel the skin off, then cut in half lengthways.

Heat the olive oil in a pan and start to fry the potatoes, after 2 minutes add the garlic and continue to fry on high heat for a further 5 minutes, stirring and moving the potatoes so they don't stick but become slightly coloured.

Remove the potatoes from the heat and stir through the herbs, let stand for a minute or two and season to taste. Serve immediately.

INGREDIENTS

600g of new potatoes
1 clove of crushed garlic
1 tbls of chopped fresh dill
1 tbls of chopped fresh parsley
½ tbls of chopped fresh mint
3 tbls of olive oil
Salt and pepper

Serves 4

£2.50

Moroccan Spiced Vegetables

Bring a pan of water to the boil, then peel and slice the carrots about 2cm thick, place into the pan and cook rapidly for 2–3 minutes. Remove the carrots with a slotted spoon and set aside.

In the same pan cook the cauliflower for 2–3 minutes, remove and set aside with the carrots.

Peel and dice the butternut squash then de-seed and dice the pepper and put all of the vegetables into an oven proof dish.

Top and tail the aubergine, slice it lengthways about 2cms thick, then dice into 2cm chunks adding to the rest of the vegetables. Add the olive oil, ground cumin, chilli powder and cinnamon to the vegetables, mix well with your hands, then bake in a pre-heated oven at gas mark 7 for about 20–25 minutes checking and stirring from time to time. Remove and serve with the rice.

INGREDIENTS

2 carrots
½ a butternut squash
1 green pepper
1 aubergine
4 cauliflower florets
4 tbls of olive oil
1 tbls of ground cumin
½ a tsp of chilli powder
1 tsp of ground cinnamon
1 tbls of chopped, fresh coriander
Salt and pepper
3 small cups of organic long grain rice cooked using the instructions on the pack

Serves 4

£4.50

Potato, Chickpea and Broad Bean Salad

Place the potatoes into a pan of cold water and bring to the boil, then turn down the heat and simmer for about 15 – 20 minutes until only just cooked. When cooked, place the pan into the sink under cold running water to cool them down and stop them cooking any further.

While the potatoes are cooking, open the chickpeas and broad beans and rinse them in a colander under cold running water. When the potatoes are cool, slice them in half lengthways and place into a bowl along with the beans and chickpeas. Now peel and finely slice the red onion, adding to the bowl. Add the juice and the olive oil, and then stir through the coriander, season according to your taste and serve.

INGREDIENTS

400g new potatoes
1 can of chickpeas
1 can of broad beans
1 red onion
4 tbls of olive oil
Juice from 2 oranges
2 tbls of chopped fresh coriander
Salt and pepper

Serves 4

23.00

Stir Fried Vegetables

Bring a large pan of water to a rapid boil, peel and slice the carrots at an angle about 1cm thick and place them into the water. Cook for about 2–3 minutes until slightly tender but still a little crisp. When cooked remove from the pan with a slotted spoon and set aside.

The next step is to remove the florets from the cauliflower and when the water is back to a rapid boil place them in the pan and cook for 2–3 minutes, then remove and set aside. Repeat the process with the broccoli.

When all the vegetables are cooked, peel and slice the onion, heat the oil in a frying pan and fry the onions and garlic. After a couple of minutes, add the rest of the vegetables and stir fry for about 2 minutes on a high heat. Add the spices and continue to stir fry for a further 3 minutes. Season according to your taste and serve.

INGREDIENTS

1 small head of broccoli
1 small head of cauliflower
2 large carrots
1 red onion
1 tsp of cumin seeds
1 tsp of ground cumin
1 tsp of ground coriander
1 clove of crushed garlic
3 tbls of olive oil
Salt and pepper

Serves 4

22.50

Tandoori Potatoes

Place the potatoes into a pan of cold water, bring to the boil, then turn down the heat and simmer for about 15–20 minutes until only just cooked. When cooked take off the heat and drain until slightly cooled, then cut the potatoes in half lengthways and set aside.

In a bowl mix the tandoori paste and the yoghurt, then heat a frying pan with the oil and start to fry the potatoes, when slightly coloured add the tandoori and yoghurt mixture and continue to cook for 1–2 minutes on a high heat, then remove from the heat and stir through the lemon juice and coriander. Finely slice the spring onions and stir through, then season with salt if needed.

INGREDIENTS

600g of new potatoes
3 tbls of tandoori paste
(ready mixed jars are fine)
5 spring onions
2 tbls of natural plain yoghurt
Juice from 1/2 a lemon
2 tbls of fresh, chopped coriander
3 tbls of vegetable oil
Salt

Serves 4

£2.20

MAIN COURSES

These dishes are all about the 'Can Cook' trainees and the sessions they had with our chef Tony. Here you'll find stews, curries, pasta, noodles – all meaty, fishy, spicy and oozing with flavour.

ALISON'S STUFFED CHICKEN WITH LINGUINE

JUST FOR YOU

INGREDIENTS
1 chicken breast beaten flat
30g of stilton
Knob of butter
½ a tbls of cream
1 tbls of chopped parsley
2 rashers of bacon
Olive oil
40ml of white wine
40ml of stock
1 tbls of corn flour
5 button mushrooms sliced
Salt and pepper
Linguine

£3.00

Beat and press the chicken breast until flat.

In a bowl mix together the stilton, butter, cream and parsley.
Season and spread all over the chicken breast.

Roll the chicken up and wrap the bacon around it, secure with cocktail sticks,
heat a pan with a little oil and fry the chicken until the bacon is golden all over.

Pour in the wine, stock and mushrooms, then simmer covered for about
30 minutes turning occasionally.

Blend the cornflour in a cup with a little cold water and add to the pan,
stirring until thickened. When cooked remove and keep warm.

Bring a pan of water to the boil and cook the pasta as per instructions on
packet. Serve the chicken on top of the pasta with the sauce poured over
the top.

AMY'S NORMANDY CASSEROLE

– SERVES TWO

INGREDIENTS
1 onion peeled and quartered
1 clove of garlic crushed
½ a stick of celery sliced
1 chicken breast diced
150ml of apple juice
200ml of water
1 carrot peeled and sliced
5 button mushrooms quartered
1 apple, peeled, cored and quartered
½ tin of broad beans
½ tbls of soy sauce
Olive oil
1 tbls of flour
Salt and pepper

£3.00

Heat 1 tbls of olive oil in a pan and fry the onions, garlic, celery and chicken for about 5 minutes, then sprinkle the flour into the pan, stirring constantly for 4 minutes before gradually adding the apple juice.

Bring to the boil while stirring then turn down the heat to a simmer and add the carrots and soy sauce – put a lid on the pan and gently simmer for about 30 minutes, checking now and again, adding a little water if needed.

After 40 minutes add the mushrooms, apple and broad beans, cover and cook for a further 20 minutes, check seasoning, maybe add a little black pepper and serve.

ANITA'S CHICKEN AND CHUNKY SWEET POTATO SOUP
- SERVES TWO

INGREDIENTS
1 sweet potato
1 chicken breast
1 clove of garlic, crushed
1 onion
2 tsp paprika
1/2 a tin of tomatoes
100ml of vegetable stock
1/2 carrot finely diced
1/2 red pepper diced
1 tbls of tomato purée
2 tbls of rice noodles
1 tbls of oregano
1 tbls of basil olive oil
Salt and pepper

£3.00

Peel and dice the sweet potato to about 1cm thick. Place in a pan of water, bring to the boil and simmer for about 5 minutes. Drain and set aside.

Slice the chicken into thin strips and place into a bowl with 1/2 the crushed garlic, 1 teaspoon of the paprika and a little olive oil and set aside.

To make the base of the soup, dice the onion and crush the remaining garlic and fry gently in a pan for about 5 minutes. Add the carrot and pepper and continue frying for a further 5 minutes. Stir in the tomatoes, vegetable stock and sweet potatoes and bring to the boil then simmer for 10 minutes. Add the rice noodles, oregano, basil, tomato purée and paprika. Season to taste and keep warm.

Finally, heat a little olive oil in a pan and fry the chicken for about 6 minutes until cooked through, season and serve the soup in a bowl with the chicken on top. Garnish with a little more fresh oregano.

BECKY'S SESAME SALMON NOODLES
A MEAL FOR ONE

INGREDIENTS
1 small fillet of salmon
1 tbls of sesame seeds
1 large handful of cooked egg noodles
1 red pepper deseeded and sliced
½ a red onion peeled and sliced
2 tbls of bean sprouts
2 tbls of chopped coriander
1 tsp of sesame oil
1 tsp of vegetable oil
1 inch piece of grated ginger
1 spring onion finely sliced
1 tbls of sweet chilli sauce
1 tbls of soy sauce

£2.50

Dip the top side of the salmon into the sesame seeds and fry in a hot pan with a little oil for about 4 minutes on each side. Remove and keep warm in a low oven.

Heat a pan with the vegetable oil and sesame oil and stir fry the peppers and onion for about 3 minutes. Add the ginger, bean sprouts, noodles, chilli sauce and soy sauce, continue to fry for a further 2 minutes then quickly stir in the coriander for a few seconds.

Serve, placing the noodles into the centre of a plate and the salmon on top. To finish, sprinkle the spring onions onto the salmon.

DEBBIE'S RUSTIC LAMB STEW FOR TWO

INGREDIENTS
4 tomatoes chopped
½ an aubergine cubed
1 courgette cubed
1 green pepper chopped
2 onions diced
2 cloves of garlic crushed
400g of cubed lamb
400ml of water
1 tbls of cumin
1 tbls of cinnamon
2 bay leaves
2 potatoes cubed
Salt and pepper

£5.00

Fry the onions and garlic in a little oil and then add the lamb and spices and continue to fry for a few minutes until browned.

Add the water and bay leaf. Cover and simmer for about 35–45 minutes until tender. Add a little more water if it starts to become a bit dry.

Now add all of the other ingredients and continue to cook until the vegetables are tender. Season according to your taste and serve with some green beans.

IAN'S SALMON WRAPPED IN BACON FOR YOU AND A FRIEND

INGREDIENTS
2 fillets of salmon
4 rashers of smoked bacon
8 new potatoes
1 red pepper
1 red onion
1 courgette
Olive oil
A handful of fresh basil
Salt and pepper

£4.50

Slice the salmon lengthways and wrap with the bacon, set aside.

Place the potatoes in a pan of cold water and bring to the boil then simmer for 15–20 minutes until just cooked, remove from pan and leave to cool slightly.

Heat a frying pan with a little oil and gently fry the salmon for about 4 minutes on each side, when cooked remove and keep warm. Retain the oil in the pan.

De-seed and slice the pepper, slice the onion and courgette and place into a bowl. Slice the potatoes into quarters and add to the bowl along with 2 tbls of olive oil and salt and pepper, then add to the same pan you cooked the fish in and fry for about 7–10 minutes stirring all the time.

Remove from the heat and add a handful of chopped basil leaves, then stir and serve on a plate with the salmon on top.

GEMMA'S STEAK AND COLCANNON POTATOES

INGREDIENTS
400g rump steak
6 medium potatoes cubed
Half a Savoy cabbage sliced
6 spring onions finely sliced
Knob of butter
Olive oil
2 tbls of crème fraiche
2 tbls of tarragon
Salt and pepper

£5.50

Cook the potatoes in a pan of water until tender (about 20 – 25 mins). While the potatoes are simmering away, cook the cabbage in a pan with the butter for about 5 minutes until slightly soft. When the potatoes are soft mash as fine as you can get them, mix in the cabbage, spring onions, then season and keep warm.

Heat a little oil in a pan and fry the steak until cooked (turning occasionally). When cooked add the crème fraiche and tarragon and season according to your taste.

Arrange the potatoes and cabbage mash to the centre of your serving plates and place the steak with the sauce onto the mash.

GEORGINA'S SPAGHETTI BOLOGNESE FOR TWO

INGREDIENTS
300g of mince
2 onions chopped
2 carrot diced
8 mushrooms sliced
1 glass of red wine
400g tin of tomatoes
2 tsp vegetable stock (or one cube)
Olive oil
Salt and pepper
4 tbls of chopped basil
Pasta cooked according to instructions
on the pack.

£4.50

(if you already have wine in the house)

Fry the mince and onions in a pan until the mince is browned (a couple of minutes), then add the red wine and reduce until the wine has nearly disappeared.

Add the tomatoes, carrot, mushrooms and stock and simmer for about 30 minutes stirring every now and again, adding a little water if needed. When cooked add the basil and season to taste, serve on top of the pasta.

Buy the best quality dried pasta you can find, it does make a difference.

JOANNA'S CORNED BEEF HASH WITH SPICED RED CABBAGE

FOR TWO PEOPLE

INGREDIENTS

For the Red Cabbage:
½ a red cabbage shredded
1 red onion sliced
1 cooking apple, peeled and sliced
½ a tsp of nutmeg
A pinch of ground cinnamon
A pinch of ground cloves
1 tbls of soft brown sugar
2 tbls of white wine vinegar
Knob of butter
1 big tbls of redcurrant jelly

For the Hash:
2 large potatoes, peeled and diced
2 small onions diced
A splash of Worcester sauce
½ a leek washed and sliced
½ a carrot peeled and sliced
200g of corned beef, chopped

£4.00

For the corned beef hash:

Place the carrot and potato into a large pan, cover with water and boil, stirring occasionally until they are cooked and soft. Drain and lightly crush.

Add the onion and leek to a frying pan with a little oil and fry for 5 minutes. Add them to the carrot and potato cooked earlier, together with the corned beef. Sprinkle in the Worcester sauce and season according to your taste.

Flour your hands and mould the mix into two large patties. Fry, turning once, over a medium heat for about 7 – 10 minutes. Serve with the red cabbage.

This is also great with a dollop of red sauce – great comfort food

For the spiced red cabbage:

Place all the ingredients (except the redcurrant jelly) into a large pan and bring to the boil. Cover and simmer for about 1 hour or until the cabbage is tender. Season well with salt and pepper and stir through the red currant jelly. Leave to stand for a couple of minutes and serve. Also works a treat with Pearl's Scouse dish (see page 75).

LISA'S CHILLI BEEF NOODLES FOR TWO

INGREDIENTS
200g of rump steak
200g of cooked egg noodles
2 tsp of grated ginger
1 clove of crushed garlic
2 tsp of sesame seeds
2 tsp of sesame oil
2 tbls of vegetable oil
1/2 a red pepper
1/2 a red onion
4 tbls of bean sprouts
2 tbls of soy sauce
2 tbls of sweet chilli sauce
1 tsp of Chinese 5 spice

£3.20

Slice the steak, onion and pepper into thin strips. Heat a frying pan until very hot then add both oils and stir fry the steak for about 1 minute before adding the pepper and onion. Continue to fry for 2 minutes.

Add the ginger, garlic, soy sauce, sweet chilli sauce, 5 spice and bean sprouts. Cook for 2 minutes then add the noodles and sesame seeds and cook for a further 2 minutes and serve.

Take care when frying with a really hot pan – the oil can spit and burn.

LORRAINE'S CHILLI CON CARNE FOR TWO

INGREDIENTS
250g of mince
2 onions chopped
1 clove of garlic
1 tbls of olive oil
2 tsp of chilli powder
1 tsp of ground cumin
8 sun dried tomatoes chopped
1 glass of red wine
1 tsp of cinnamon
1 can of kidney beans drained
1 tin of tomatoes
Salt and pepper
Long grain rice

£3.50

(if you already have red wine in the house)

Fry the onions and mince in a pan until the mince is browned. Add the wine and cook until nearly all the wine has been absorbed.

Add the spices and garlic and cook for 2 minutes before adding all of the remaining ingredients except the kidney beans. Cook for 35 minutes stirring now and again adding a little water if needed.

After 20 minutes add the kidney beans and cook for a further 15 minutes. Season according to your taste and serve with rice and / or tortilla chips.

LYNDSEY'S SALMON WITH DILL AND SPRING ONION MASH FOR TWO

INGREDIENTS
2 fillets of salmon
Zest and juice from 1 lemon
1 tbls of chopped dill
Salt and pepper
4 medium potatoes peeled and chopped
Knob of butter
6 tbls of cream
8 spring onions finely sliced
2 tbls of chopped chives

£4.50

Place the salmon into a bowl along with the dill, zest and juice from the lemon and season.

Put the potatoes into a pan of cold water and bring to the boil, then simmer for about 20 – 25 minutes until cooked. Remove from pan and mash as fine and smooth as you can. Put the mashed potato back into the pan, add the cream and butter and mix well. Season to taste and keep warm.

Heat a little oil in a pan and fry the salmon for about 4 minutes on each side. Remove and keep warm. Stir the spring onions and chives into the mash and serve onto the centre of your serving plate with the salmon on top.

THE CAN COOK WILL COOK BARBEQUE

Weather permitting (and we got lucky), a barbie provides the ideal place for simple, fresh food that's ready to go in minutes and can be set up almost anywhere you have a bit of outside space – we borrowed a bit of a local park to celebrate the end of our training with our trainees.

Look at the weather forecast, pick a day, take a bit of time to prepare our recipes and let the food take centre stage.

BBQ BEEFBURGERS

Finely chop or grate the onion and crush the garlic. Heat a little oil in a pan and gently fry the onion and garlic for about 5 minutes until soft but not too coloured, leave to cool.

In a bowl start to squeeze the mince with your hands until it becomes soft and well mixed, then add the paprika, mixed herbs, tomato purée and salt and pepper and combine well.

When the onion mixture has cooled add to the mince and squeeze and scrunch again until everything is well combined. Now shape the mixture into a burger shape and place onto an oiled plate and refrigerate for about 10 minutes.

Heat a little oil in a frying pan and fry the burger for about 4 minutes on each side until cooked and serve in the burger bun along with the lettuce, tomato, cheese and sauce if using.

Makes 10 burgers.

INGREDIENTS
670g minced beef
4 white onions
4 cloves of garlic
1/4 tsp paprika
8 tsp mixed herbs
8 tsp tomato purée
3 tsp salt
4 tsp pepper
10 burger buns
10 slices of cheese
20 slices of tomato
Lettuce

BBQ CHICKEN KEBABS

In a bowl mix all of the ingredients together, cover and refrigerate for at least 2 hours or preferably overnight.

When the chicken has marinated skewer the chicken and onion onto the wooden skewers – there should be enough for 4 skewers.

Cook them on the barbie for about 10 – 20 minutes depending on how thick you sliced the chicken and how hot the barbie is.

INGREDIENTS
2 chicken breasts sliced lengthways
2 tsp of ground cumin
1 clove of garlic crushed
Juice from 1 lemon
1 tbls of honey
1 tbls of soy sauce
2 tbls of chopped coriander
1 red onion peeled and cut into 8
4 wooden skewers
1 tsp black pepper

BBQ WHOLE SEA BASS

Lay out the foil on a table and place half the sliced lemons in a line along the middle then lay the fish on top.

Using a sharp knife make a few slices into the fish on both sides, then rub the fennel, olive oil, salt and pepper and lemon juice into the cuts.

Place the dill into the cavity, now bring all four sides of the foil upwards and scrunch together to make something that looks like a bag. Place the fish onto the hottest part of the barbie and cook for 15 – 20 minutes in the foil.

INGREDIENTS
1 whole sea bass gutted and scaled
1 lemon sliced plus the juice from 1 more
A few sprigs of fresh dill
1 tsp of crushed fennel seeds
Pinch of salt and black pepper
2 tbls of olive oil
Enough silver foil to wrap the fish in

MARCELLA'S SWEET AND TANGY CHICKEN
FOR TWO HUNGRY PEOPLE OR A LIGHT LUNCH FOR FOUR

INGREDIENTS
2 chicken breasts cut into strips
1 onion diced
1 red pepper sliced
100ml of water
400g tin of chopped tomatoes
½ a can of pineapple cubes and
the juice from the can
1 clove of garlic
1 carrot finely sliced
2 tbls of sweet chilli sauce
2 tsp of tomato purée
2 tbls of olive oil
Cooked rice to serve

£4.00

Heat a pan with the olive oil and fry the chicken and onion for about 5 minutes before adding the garlic, pepper, carrot, chilli sauce, tomatoes and pineapple juice. Cook for a further 5 minutes.

Now add the tomato purée and pineapple cubes and cook for a further 2 minutes. Season according to your taste and serve with rice.

MARIA'S CHICKEN CURRY FOR TWO

INGREDIENTS
4 tomatoes
1 medium onion
3 tbls of vegetable oil
2 tsp of grated root ginger
2 small clove of garlic crushed
2 green chillis
1 tsp of chilli powder
1 tsp of ground coriander
1 tsp of ground cumin
1 tsp of ground turmeric
1 chicken breast
2 large handfuls of spinach
$\frac{1}{2}$ a can of green lentils
200ml of coconut milk
Salt and pepper

£3.50

Peel and dice the onion and fry over a low heat for 7 – 10 minutes until soft, coloured but not burnt.

De-seed the tomatoes and chilli, and chop them both. Put the oil into the frying pan, add all the dry spices and the onions and fry for 2 minutes stirring continuously. Next, add the chilli, tomatoes, ginger and garlic, and fry for a further minute. At this point add a touch of salt.

Now add the chicken and fry for 1 minute, tossing the chicken as it cooks. Pour in the coconut milk, stir and bring to the boil. Simmer gently for about 20 minutes.

After 20 minutes add the drained and washed lentils and spinach, and cook for a further 5 minutes. Season according to your taste. Serve with warm naan bread and pilau rice.

MARY'S KEDGEREE - A NICE LUNCH FOR TWO

INGREDIENTS
75g of brown basmati rice
35g of puy lentils
Pinch of turmeric
½ an onion finely chopped
½ a tsp of ground cumin
½ a tsp of ground coriander
1½ tbls of olive oil
250g of smoked haddock sliced thickly
2 eggs
3 tbls of fresh, coriander chopped

£4.50

SPECIAL EQUIPMENT
You will need a fairly big frying pan for this dish

Place the rice and lentils in a saucepan and add about 250ml of boiling water. Add the turmeric and give the rice and lentils a good stir. Cover with a lid and bring to the boil, then gently simmer for about 20–25 minutes until the rice is just cooked and the lentils are soft. Remove from the heat and leave with the lid on to steam for another 10 minutes or so. If there is still water in the pan cook gently until it has evaporated.

On a low to medium heat, fry the onion, cumin and ground coriander in the oil for about 10 minutes, until soft and translucent. Increase the heat to high and add the haddock and cook for a few minutes. When the haddock is just cooked push to one side of the pan and crack the eggs into the pan. Cook until the whites start to turn solid and break the yolks so they cook quicker (like a scrambled egg). When the eggs are just cooked, briefly stir into the haddock mixture trying to leave some big pieces of egg if you can.

Add the rice mixture to the pan with half the chopped coriander and stir just enough to mix together and warm the rice. Season to taste and serve with the remaining coriander on top.

MICK'S LAMB CURRY FOR TWO HUNGRY PEOPLE AFTER A GOOD NIGHT OUT

INGREDIENTS
400g of diced lamb
4 tbls of vegetable oil
2 tsp of grated ginger
2 cloves of crushed garlic
1 tsp of turmeric
3 tsp of garam masala
2 tsp of ground coriander
2 tsp of ground cumin
2 tbls of plain yoghurt
2 tsp of chilli powder
2 onions finely chopped
1 can of chopped tomatoes
200ml of water
4 tbls of chopped, fresh coriander
Salt and pepper
3 small cups of basmati rice cooked following
instructions on the pack
Naan bread

£4.50

Fry the onion in the oil for about 5 minutes on a medium heat, then add the ginger and garlic and fry for a further minute before adding all the dry spices and the lamb. Continue frying for another 3 minutes adding a little salt.

Now stir in the tinned tomatoes, add some water, cover the pan and simmer, stirring from time to time, adding more water if needed. After 45 minutes, add the yoghurt and fresh coriander and cook for 2 minutes. Season according to your taste, serve with basmati rice and of course a naan.

NICKIE'S WARM DUCK SALAD FOR TWO
(AS A STARTER)

INGREDIENTS
1 duck breast
1 tbls of soy sauce
1 tsp of Chinese five spice
Juice from ½ an orange
A dash of sesame oil
1 tbls of vegetable oil
½ a yellow pepper
4 cherry tomatoes
1 carrot
2 tbls of bean sprouts
A handful of mixed salad leaves

£4.00

Peel the skin off the duck breast and place the duck into a bowl along with the soy, 5 spice, sesame oil and orange juice. Leave to marinate for about 20 minutes.

Heat a little oil in a frying pan and add the duck to the pan when warm (not too hot or the marinade will burn). Gently fry for about 4 minutes on each side, remove and keep warm.

De-seed and finely slice the yellow pepper, slice the tomatoes into quarters and add to a bowl along with the salad leaves. Peel the carrot and then using the peeler shave the flesh of the carrot into the bowl and add the bean sprouts.

Serve the salad on a plate, slice the duck and place on top then drizzle the juice over the top.

NICOLA'S LAMB STEW WITH WHITE CABBAGE FOR TWO

INGREDIENTS
400g of cubed lamb (shoulder)
2 knobs of butter
2 tsp of salt
1 tsp of black pepper
1 tsp of ground cinnamon
2 tsp of ground cumin
2 tsp of paprika
2 onions sliced
¼ white cabbage sliced
2 carrots sliced
2 tbls of sugar
500ml of water

£4.00

Heat a pan, add the butter and fry the onion and lamb. As the lamb changes colour add the spices and cook for a minute or so. Sprinkle on the sugar and then add all the other ingredients.

Bring the stew to the boil, cover and simmer for about 50 – 60 minutes, stirring from time to time and adding a little water if needed.

Season to taste and serve with a hearty portion of spring onion mash.
(See page 56 for recipe)

PEARL'S REAL LIVERPUDLIAN SCOUSE FOR A FAMILY OF FOUR

INGREDIENTS
4 tbls of vegetable oil
600g of chuck steak
1 onion chopped
2 carrots peeled and chopped
3 small leeks sliced
2 large potatoes diced
1ltr of beef stock
6 tbls of flour
Salt and pepper
3 tsp of Worcester sauce

£4.50

Cut the steak into chunks, season with salt, coat in the flour and pat off any excess.

Heat a large pan with a little oil and fry the steak until browned. Stir continually to prevent the steak from sticking to the pan. Add the stock and the rest of the vegetables, cover and simmer for about 1 hour or until meat is tender. Keep checking and add more water if it starts to dry towards the end of the hour.

Season according to your taste. We like it with lots of black pepper, particularly on cold nights. Serve with warm buttered bread. This really works with spiced red cabbage. (See page 51 for recipe).

REBECCA'S SINGAPORE FRIED NOODLES FOR TWO

INGREDIENTS
30g of cashew nuts
½ a tsp of coriander seeds
½ a tsp of cumin seeds
½ a tsp of chilli powder
4 tbls of groundnut oil
250ml of coconut milk
140g of rice noodles
1 chicken breast
2 small red chillis
4 spring onions
2 tomatoes
100g of tofu
Salt and pepper
A large handful of fresh coriander

£3.50

NOTES
You will need a large frying pan or wok for this dish.
Use ready cooked noodles to make things easier.

Put the cashew nuts, coriander seeds, cumin seeds and chilli powder into a pestle and mortar and pound until everything is ground up. Heat half the oil in a frying pan and fry the spice mixture for 1 minute. Slowly stir in the coconut milk, bring to the boil and simmer for 5 minutes then set aside.

As the coconut milk simmers, place the rice noodles into a bowl, cover with boiling water and leave to stand for 2 – 3 minutes. Drain the noodles and leave to stand.

Cut the chicken into strips. Core, de-seed and chop the chilli. Slice the spring onions and roughly chop the tomato. Drain the tofu and cut into 3cm cubes. Heat the remaining oil in a frying pan and stir fry the chicken for 3 minutes or until browned. Add the chilli and spring onions and stir fry for a further 2 minutes.

Add the roughly chopped tomato, diced tofu, the rice noodles and coconut mixture to the pan and stir fry for another 2 minutes or until the whole thing is heated through. Season to your taste with salt and pepper. Roughly chop the fresh coriander, sprinkle over the top and serve.

STACEY'S SALMON WITH ROCKET AND CRUSHED POTATOES - A QUICK MEAL FOR YOU

INGREDIENTS
200g of salmon fillet
200g of new potatoes
3 spring onions
1 tbls of fresh chopped dill
A small handful of rocket leaves
1 tsp smoked paprika
Juice from 1/2 a lemon
3 tbls of olive oil
Salt and pepper

£2.50

Place the potatoes into a pan of cold water and bring to the boil then simmer with the lid on for about 15 – 20 minutes until just tender.

While the potatoes are cooking, slice the salmon in half, length ways, place into a bowl along with the paprika, lemon juice, 1 tbls of olive oil and a pinch of salt and pepper. Gently rub it all into the fish and set aside.

When the potatoes are cooked, drain and crush with a fork, then finely slice the spring onions and add to the potatoes along with the dill, rocket and the remaining olive oil. Season and mix well, then keep warm.

Heat a pan with a little olive oil and cook the salmon for about 1 – 2 minutes on each side, then serve the potatoes on a plate with the salmon on top.

SAMANTHA'S BALSAMIC CHICKEN AND HERBY POTATOES FOR TWO

INGREDIENTS
2 chicken breasts
2 tbls of balsamic vinegar
2 tbls of honey
2 tbls of wholegrain mustard
2 cloves of garlic crushed
400g of new potatoes
2 tbls of chopped tarragon
2 tbls of chopped parsley
Salt and pepper
2 handfuls of watercress
1 lemon

Slice each chicken breast into 3 pieces and put into a bowl along with the balsamic vinegar, honey, mustard and garlic. Mix well, then set aside.

Place the potatoes into a pan with enough cold water to cover them, bring to the boil and simmer for about 15 – 20 minutes or until tender. Drain and allow them to cool slightly. When cool enough to handle, peel the skins off and slice in half then set aside.

Heat a frying pan with a little oil, take the chicken breast out of the marinade and fry for about 5 minutes on each side until cooked. Take off the heat, season with salt and pepper and leave in the pan to keep warm.

Heat another frying pan with 2 tablespoons of olive oil and fry the potatoes for about 5 minutes until slightly coloured and heated through. Add the chopped tarragon and parsley and the juice from half the lemon. Season to your taste.

Squeeze the juice from the other half of the lemon over the watercress and serve all three together.

TONY'S NAN'S MEATBALLS

– SERVES FOUR FOR LUNCH

INGREDIENTS
500g of lean minced beef
2 onions
2 cloves of garlic crushed
1 tbls of dry basil
2 tbls of chopped fresh oregano
2 tbls of chopped fresh basil
2 tins of chopped plum tomatoes
Olive oil
1 tsp of sugar
Salt and pepper
Egg pasta cooked following the
instructions on the pack

£4.50

Peel and very finely dice the onions. Heat a frying pan with a little olive oil and gently fry one of the onions until soft for about 5 minutes then set aside.

In a large pan, heat a little olive oil and fry the other onion and 1 clove of garlic until they start to colour, then add the chopped tomatoes, sugar and dry basil. Bring to a gentle simmer and leave for about 20 minutes stirring from time to time. Add a little water if needed.

In a large bowl, mix the mince, the onion we cooked first, 1 chopped clove of garlic, the fresh herbs, 1 tsp of salt and ½ tsp pepper. Squash everything together with your hands until it's all combined well. Mould the mixture into balls by rolling it in your hands. They should be a little bigger than golf balls.

Heat a frying pan with a little olive oil and fry the meatballs just enough to colour, then add them to the tomato sauce, cover and simmer for 20 – 25 minutes. Season the tomato sauce to your taste and serve on a nice bed of pasta. You could add a little parmesan cheese to this.

DESSERTS

Everyone has a childhood favourite.
Here are some of ours.

Bakewell Tart

Making the pastry
Roll out the pastry and press into a 4 inch loose bottom flan dish or until it's about as thick as a pound coin throughout. Prick the pastry base with a fork and chill for 20 minutes in the fridge.

Line the pastry with greaseproof paper, pour the rice onto the paper then bake in the oven on gas mark 4 for about 20 minutes (the weight of the rice stops the pastry puffing up). After 20 minutes, remove from the oven, remove the greaseproof paper and rice and let it cool down.

Making the frangipane mix
Combine the butter and sugar in a bowl until smooth. Add the ground almonds and blend together. Add the cornflour and flour, then add the egg and egg white and mix until very smooth. Add in the vanilla and almond extract to bind.

To finish off...
Spread a little jam over the bottom of the pastry case, add the frangipane mix on top and bake in the oven for about 30 minutes until the frangipane is puffed, golden brown and firm to the touch.

INGREDIENTS
80g of soft butter
130g of caster sugar
½ a cup of ground almonds
1 tsp of cornflour
2 tsp of flour
1 egg
1 egg white
1 tsp of vanilla extract
2 tsp of almond extract
Raspberry jam
1 pack of shortcrust pastry

ADDITIONAL EQUIPMENT
A loose based flan dish
Greasproof paper
A cup of rice to use as a weight

£3.00

STICKY TOFFEE PUDDING DAY

Sticky toffee pudding has always been a firm favorite in our cafés. We had lots of requests to put the recipe into the book. So we thought, lets make a day of it (well an afternoon really) and get a few mums and their children in to all have a go and make some puds.

The Cast
Jenny and Ellie – Jenny is a midwife at our centre.
Angie, Cindy, Toni and David – Angie works in our cafés and had hardly cooked before joining us.
Liz, Will and Lilly – Liz is the understanding wife of Tony our chef (you see, chefs work long hours)

If you can find a bit of space, try your own sticky toffee session – the kids love it.

For the pudding

Place the dates into a pan and add the water, put onto a medium heat until the dates have softened. Remove from the heat and blend until smooth. Set the dates aside.

In a large bowl mix together the butter and sugar until light and fluffy using a wooden spoon or an electric whisk if you have one, then add the eggs one by one mixing all the time. Add the flour, baking powder, bicarbonate of soda, golden syrup and puréed dates and combine well.

Grease and flour 4 moulds, divide the mixture between them and bake in a preheated oven gas mark 6 for 20 – 25 minutes until firm to the touch.

For the sauce

Melt the butter in a pan and stir in the sugar and syrup, then add the double cream and bring to the boil, whisk well and remove from the heat ready to use.

INGREDIENTS

For the pudding:
180g of soft dark brown sugar
60g of soft butter
2 eggs
200g of flour
200g of dried pitted dates
3 tbls of golden syrup
300ml of boiling water
1 tsp of baking powder
1 tsp of bicarbonate of soda

For the sauce:
150ml of double cream
60g of butter
60g of soft dark brown sugar
2 tbls of golden syrup

£3.00

(makes about 6 puddings)

ADDITIONAL EQUIPMENT

Food processor or hand blender to make the date purée.
Electric whisk (optional)

Simple Rice Pudding

Put all the ingredients into a pan and bring to a gentle simmer.
Cover with a lid and leave to simmer until the milk has been absorbed
and the rice is cooked. It's that easy.

INGREDIENTS
25g of butter
60g of caster sugar
1 pint of milk
1 tsp of vanilla extract
70g of pudding rice

Serves 4

Chocolate Orange Mousse

Break the chocolate into small pieces and place in a bowl over a pan of simmering water, let the chocolate melt slowly. While the chocolate is melting, whip the cream until it forms soft peaks and set aside.

Once the chocolate has melted, remove from the heat and let it cool slightly, then beat in the egg yolks. Once the egg yolks are mixed in fold in the double cream, and then whisk the egg whites to form stiff peaks, fold the orange zest, pour into small glasses and chill for at least 2 hours in your fridge.

How to separate an egg.
Break the egg into the palm of your hand and let the egg white fall through your fingers into a bowl – messy we know, but its fun and it works.

INGREDIENTS
130g of dark chocolate
130ml of double cream
2 eggs (separated, yolks and whites)
2 tsp of orange zest

Serves 2 – 4

£2.50

SANDWICHES

The staple solution for almost everyone who's in a hurry. Slow down and try these with friends, family or just as you ponder your day.

Steak and Caramelised Onion Baguette

Peel and slice the onion and place in a pan along with the sugar and vinegar and cook on a really low heat for about 1 hour, stirring from time to time. You want the onions to be soft and very sticky but not burnt.

Heat a pan with a little oil and fry the steak to your liking. Set aside once cooked. Slice the baguette in half lengthways and lightly toast. Mix the mayonnaise with both mustards and spread over the baguette.

Take the steak and slice at an angle into bite size pieces. Arrange the steak on the baguettes and cover with the onions. Season according to your taste.

INGREDIENTS
3 white onions
6 tbls of white wine vinegar
3 tbls of soft dark brown sugar
4 baguettes
4 x 100g of rump steak
Salt and pepper
4 tbls of mayonnaise
2 tsp of wholegrain mustard
2 tsp of Dijon mustard

£7.00

Mature Cheddar and Roast Tomato Baguette for one

Slice the tomatoes in half and lay in an oven proof dish, then divide the basil between the four halves, sprinkle with a pinch of salt and pepper and drizzle with a little olive oil. Cook in a pre-heated oven at gas mark 2 for about 1 hour. Slice the baguette in half lengthways and lightly toast, then spread a little butter and place the cheese onto one side and the tomatoes on top, then put the lid on and serve.

This baguette is always best when serving guests as you can oven roast more tomatoes, otherwise it can be a bit costly just roasting a couple of tomatoes. Alternatively you could roast a load of tomatoes, keep them cool in the fridge and add them to cooked breakfasts or salads through the week.

INGREDIENTS
1 baguette
2 tomatoes
50g of grated mature cheddar
1 tsp of dried basil
Olive oil
Maldon sea salt
Black pepper
Butter

£1.50

Salmon Wrap with Tartare Sauce for two of you

To make the tartare sauce:
In a bowl mix together the mayonnaise, capers, gherkins, egg, dill and lemon juice then season to your taste.

Slice the salmon in half lengthways and lightly season with salt and pepper. Heat a little oil in a pan and fry the salmon for 1–2 minutes on each side, remove and keep warm in a low oven.

Spread the tartare sauce over the wrap and add the salmon, lettuce, cucumber and spring onions across the middle, then roll the wrap up to form a tube. Slice the wrap in the middle at an angle and serve.

INGREDIENTS
225g fillet of salmon
2 large tortilla wraps
8 thin slices of cucumber
2 small handfuls of shredded iceberg lettuce
4 spring onions sliced
3 tbls of mayonnaise
4 tsp of washed capers
4 tsp of chopped gherkins
Half a boiled egg chopped
1 tbls of chopped fresh dill
2 tsp of lemon juice
Salt and pepper
Olive oil

£2.95

PASTES, SAUCES + DRESSINGS

For a quick solution there are some great off the shelf versions
but if you want to spend a bit of time preparing your own
we like these and they work.

Classic salad dressing

Place the lemon juice and olive oil into a bowl and season with salt and pepper, then add the garlic and allow to infuse for 30 minutes, then remove. Now add the mustard and sugar and stir well. This will go well with salads accompanying chicken or seafood.

INGREDIENTS
2 tbls of olive oil
6 tbls of lemon juice
1 clove of garlic bruised
1 tsp of Dijon mustard
1 tsp of castor sugar
Pinch of salt
2 twists of a black pepper mill

Indian curry paste

Place all of the ingredients into a food processor and blitz into a paste. This can be used straight away or stored in a jar in the fridge for up to 3 weeks.

INGREDIENTS
2 tsp of garam masala
1 small onion peeled and chopped
2 cloves of garlic chopped
3 inch piece of root ginger peeled and chopped
3 green chillies chopped
1 tsp coriander seeds crushed
2 tomatoes deseeded and chopped
1 tsp of salt
2 tbls of groundnut oil

Thai curry paste

Place all of the ingredients into a food processor and blitz into a paste. You can use this straight away or it will keep in a sealed jar for about 3 weeks.

INGREDIENTS
5 medium green chillies deseeded
1 onion peeled and chopped
6 inch piece of root ginger peeled and chopped
2 cloves of garlic
1 small bunch of fresh coriander, stalks and all
2 lemongrass stalks chopped
Zest and juice from 1 lime
6 kaffir lime leaves (if you can't get these then replace with the zest from 1 more lime)
1 tbls of coriander seeds crushed
1 tsp of ground cumin
1 tsp of black peppercorns crushed
2 tsp of fish sauce
3 tbls of groundnut oil

Yoghurt and Cumin dressing

In a bowl mix the yogurt and lemon juice, then add the garlic and mix well to incorporate the garlic then stir through the coriander and season with salt and pepper. This dressing would go well with salads which feature meat dishes especially lamb.

INGREDIENTS
4 tbls of Greek yogurt
1 tbls of lemon juice
1/2 a clove of garlic crushed
2 tsp of ground cumin
1 tbls of chopped coriander
Pinch of salt
Pinch of black pepper

Kids Lunch boxes

The best place to start your own little '5-a-day' campaign with your children. We think it's all about encouraging healthier habits very early on in their lives. At home around the dinner table is the most important space, but when they trot off to school, the lunch box is the next best place to be. Typically, add some thinly sliced veggies and fruit to a healthy, full fruit drink, a small yogurt and, together with a meat or cheese and tomato cob, there you have it – a full colour healthy food experience, full of vitamins and not a spoon in sight.

As a suggestion try:

Handful of thinly sliced mixed peppers
I carrot again thinly sliced
2 inch piece of cucumber sliced just like the carrot
Slice and core half an apple into bite sized bits
Little bunch of grapes (we have found the kids like red best)
The cob – with your choice of sliced meat or maybe cheese and tomato
Yogurt pouch
Pomegreat drink

Tip: You can now buy lunch boxes for about £6 which have small removable ice packs in – if you can find one, these are the best because everything stays chilled throughout the day.

People we like

The Green Fish Café

Dave and his staff run the best café in Liverpool City Centre.

The Green Fish (great name) opened in 1994 and provides really affordable healthy food. The Green Fish is a really popular vegetarian oasis which also caters for gluten intolerance, dairy free and low cholesterol diets. It's so good, it became one of the first food venues to receive the Heart of Mersey award. Now, 14 years on, it still retains its unique charming atmosphere.

If you want a great lunch be sure to visit or call ahead on 0151 707 8592.

Claire Kenny

Every now and then you meet someone who really lives their job and makes an immediate first impression – Claire (who will proudly tell you she is a 1st Assistant at our local McDonald's) loves her job and was a great help when we were thinking about our cafés and how our customer service should work. McDonald's should be proud. Thanks Claire.

Fun facts and figures

During the making of this book 3 trainees gave birth. We trained 22 people – mothers, mothers to be, fathers, fathers to be, grandmothers and one granddad. We used 10 camping stoves, 10 preparation tables, some very sharp knives, brightly coloured chopping boards, pots, pans, bowls, all the necessary shiny utensils and some trendy aprons then we prepared all this food – 12 red cabbages, over 100 red onions, about 20 bunches of spring onions, 50 big carrots, sticks and sticks of celery, 40 kilos of Maris Piper potatoes, 5 kilos of baby potatoes, 70 leeks, 30 cucumbers, 2 very big boxes of tomatoes, 10 tubs of cherry tomatoes, bags of mixed peppers, 5 kilos of mushrooms, 12 courgettes, 50 chicken breasts, a couple of duck breasts, 5 kilos each of beef steak and beef mince, 8 kilos of lamb shoulder, 7 sides of salmon, a large sea bass for the barbie, 50 sardines, 10 bunches of fresh mint, 12 bunches of fresh coriander, 7 bunches of fresh dill, 10 bunches of fresh parsley, 5 bunches each of fresh basil and tarragon (which we grew ourselves), 3 bunches of thyme, 15 bulging bulbs of garlic, 40 lemons, various cheeses, 20 tins of chickpeas, 15 tins of kidney beans, 12 tins of borlotti beans, bags and bags of egg noodles, pasta of varying shapes and sizes, kilos of organic rice, good quality veg and chicken stock, approximately 8 litres of olive oil, a few litres of veg oil, a bottle or two of balsamic vinegar, bottles of red and white wine, 2 bottles of Worcester sauce, 3 bottles of soy sauce, 3 litres of cream, tubs of yogurt, 5 tins of coconut milk, a large catering box of eggs, 20 kilos of plain flour, 4 bottles of white wine vinegar, lots of salt, pepper, nutmeg, cinnamon, garam masala, ground cloves, chilli powder, paprika, cumin, turmeric, coriander powder, mustard, honey and all those other bits that add bite.

ROBBIE

TONY

MIKE

ALEX

Credits

Can Cook Will Cook concept: **Robbie Davison** (robbie.davison@surestartspeke.org)
Chef: **Tony Evans** (tony.evans@surestartspeke.org)
Design: **Mike Carney / Mike's Studio** (www.mikesstudio.co.uk)
Photography: **Alexandra Wolkowicz** (www.wolkowicz.com)
Additional photography: Mike and Robbie.

Supporters

Susan Roberts, Director, Sure Start Speke (susan.roberts@surestartspeke.org)
Mark Ord, Director, Speke Training and Education Centre (mark@stecltd.mersinet.co.uk)
Julie Curren, Food and Health Co-ordinator, Liverpool Primary Care Trust (julie.curren@liverpoolpct.nhs.uk)
Irene Mills, Public Health Neighbourhood Manager (irene.mills@liverpoolpct.nhs.uk)
Fiona Shaw, Director, Capsica (www.loveliverpoolbooks.com)
Jo Norton, Community Engagement Officer, (nortonj175@yahoo.co.uk)

First published in September 2007
Published by Pepper Books, an imprint of Capsica
83 Ampthill Road, Liverpool L17 9QN

Sure Start Speke, Children's Centre,
Conleach Road, Speke, Liverpool L24 0TW
www.surestartspeke.org

A CIP Catalogue record for this book is available from the British Library
ISBN 978-0-955654725

All proceeds from this book go towards developing services for children and families.

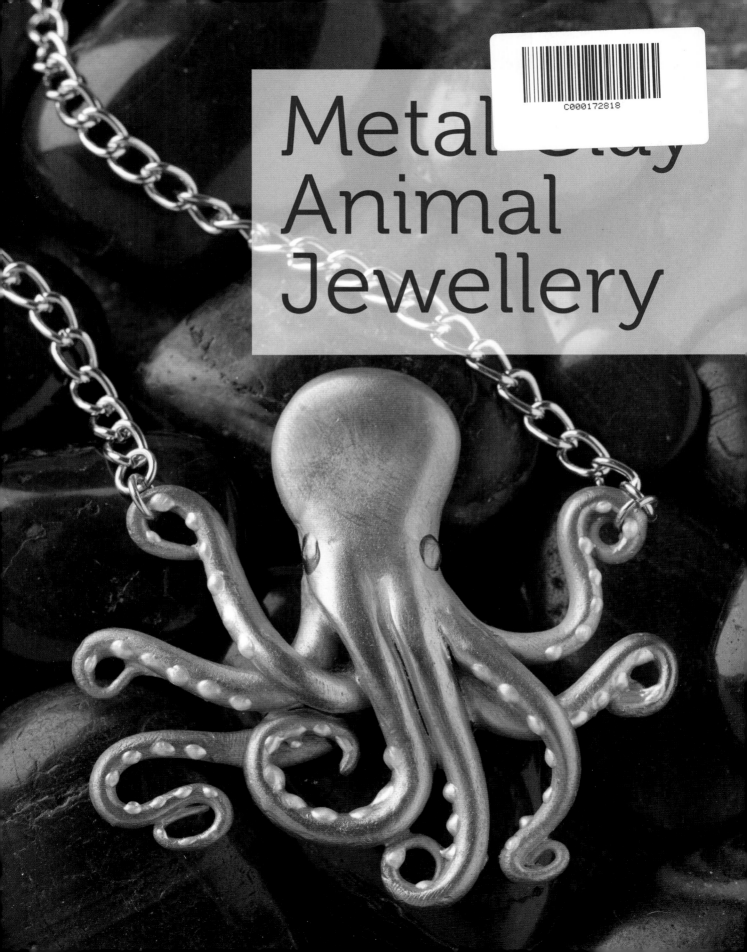

Metal Clay
Animal
Jewellery

Dedication

To Estella, my most perfect creation.

Acknowledgements

Thank you to Search Press for being such a fantastic publisher to work with and to all the team who contributed to each stage in the process of getting this book out into the world.

A big thank you to my editor Becky Shackleton for being as patient and supportive as ever and for helping me arrange my thoughts and ideas clearly. I am so appreciative of Paul Bricknell's beautiful photography and the artistry of Juan Hayward, in the styling of the jewellery photographs and design layout of this book.

I would like to express my sincere thanks to Louise MacLeod of Bead House, for kindly supplying the beads and jewellery making materials for the projects in this book.

I would not have been able to complete this book without the love, support and encouragement of my beautiful daughter Estella and my dearest friend Tracy McElroy. You are my biggest cheerleaders and I am thankful for this every day.

Finally, my biggest thanks go to you for buying and reading this book. I love being creative, so thank you for enabling me to continue doing what I love every day.

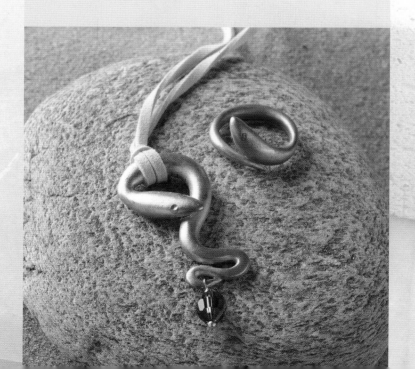

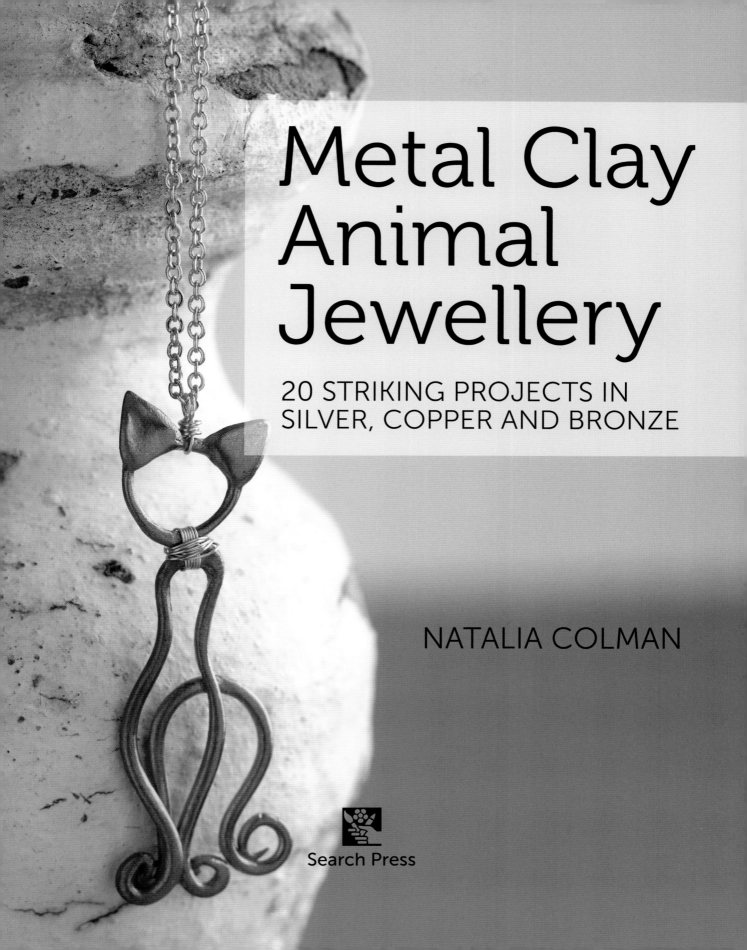

Metal Clay
Animal
Jewellery

20 STRIKING PROJECTS IN SILVER, COPPER AND BRONZE

NATALIA COLMAN

Search Press

First published in 2016

Search Press Limited
Wellwood, North Farm Road,
Tunbridge Wells, Kent TN2 3DR

Illustrations and text copyright © Natalia Colman, 2016

Photographs by Paul Bricknell at Search Press Studios

Photographs and design copyright © Search Press Ltd. 2016

ISBN: 978-1-78221-077-1

The Publishers and author can accept no responsibility for any consequences arising from the information, advice or instructions given in this publication.

Suppliers
If you have difficulty in obtaining any of the materials and equipment mentioned in this book, please visit the Search Press website for details of suppliers:
www.searchpress.com

You are invited to visit the author's website:
www.bynatalia.co.uk

Printed in China

Contents

Introduction

Metal clays are one of the most miraculous advancements in jewellery making of the 20th century. It is hard to believe that tiny particles of precious metals combined with water and a special binding agent can be converted into a metal clay that feels and behaves in a similar way to ceramic clay. This clay can be rolled, moulded, sculpted and textured, then with a few simple firing techniques, is transformed into a solid piece of precious metal.

Through the information and projects in this book, I hope to show you the incredible qualities of silver, copper and bronze clays and how they can be used most effectively to create beautiful pieces of jewellery. Throughout this book I have been inspired by Mother Nature, and every design is based on a beautiful creature or a member of the animal kingdom.

Animals have inspired jewellery designers throughout history, from the Ancient Egyptians right through to the modern day. I had so much fun coming up with my own ideas about how to represent these amazing creatures in bronze, copper and silver. I hope they inspire you to make them and add your own design flair. The designs here range from those that use quite simple techniques through to projects that are more complex. Each project is fully illustrated and all the steps are explained in detail to enable you to complete each one with confidence. So whether you are a novice jewellery maker or more experienced in working with metal clays, you will find the advice, ideas and inspiration you need. I hope you enjoy my book and that you have as much fun making these pieces as I did.

Clays

Precious metal clays contain three components: minute particles of pure precious metal, held together with water and a special binding ingredient. The only difference between the clays is the precious metal that is used and the specific binding agent for each metal. Metals that could once only be worked by hammering, sawing, piercing and melting can now be sculpted, rolled, shaped and carved, just like ceramic clay. When the water has evaporated from the clay and it has been fired for the correct length of time at the right temperature, the particles melt together to form a piece of precious metal. A fired precious metal clay piece is never quite as strong as sheet metal or metal that has been melted down, but it looks and feels exactly the same as a traditional precious metal.

Silver clay

There are eight noble metals in existence. These metals do not corrode and are resistant to oxidisation in moist air. The noble metals are considered to be the most precious metals of all due to their rarity, and silver is one of these.

Silver clay is my favourite metal clay to work with because of these noble qualities. The firing of it is also much simpler than other metal clays and there is no threat of the metal oxidising before, during or after firing. Continuous development by silver clay manufacturers has given us a lot of advancements. The early silver clay products had a shrinkage rate of 30 per cent. Those available on the market today shrink by just 6–8 per cent. These modern silver clays can be fired with a gas torch, on wire mesh on top of a gas stove or in a kiln. When the silver clay has been fired, it has a silver content of 99.9 per cent and is referred to as 'fine silver'. This is the purest form of silver that exists; sterling silver contains copper or has other metals mixed with it and has a silver content of 92.5 per cent. In the UK, it is a legal requirement to hallmark any individual piece of silver that is sold weighing above the weight of 7.78g ($^1/_3$OZ). The Assay Office will hallmark sterling silver with the numbers '925'. Fine silver is hallmarked '999'.

SILVER CLAY MANUFACTURERS

At the time of writing this book there are two leading manufacturers of silver clay, both of which are Japanese. The first is Mitsubishi Materials, which originally invented silver clay. Their product is called PMC (which stands for Precious Metal Clay). The second is Aida Industries, which manufactures silver clay under the brand name Art Clay Silver. Inside each packet of clay there are instructions from the manufacturer about working with, drying and firing their particular product. On pages 168–169 I have recommended firing methods and temperatures that will apply to both PMC and Art Clay Silver when making the projects in this book.

LUMP CLAY

This is the name given to mouldable silver clay that resembles ceramic clay. All of the projects in this book are created using lump clay. Lump clay is the perfect medium for jewellery making because it can be sculpted with your hands or modelling tools, rolled, shaped and textured. When it has dried you can continue to work on the clay. You can etch into it, carve it, layer it, sand it and re-wet it. If you like you can even grind it down into a powder, add water and make it into a paste or reconstitute it back into lump clay. When the clay is dry it is brittle, so you need to take care when working with it to avoid breaking it before it is fired.

There are two new developments in PMC lump clay, called PMC Flex and PMC Sterling. PMC Flex is a special formula of silver clay that remains flexible after it has dried. It still contains 99.9 per cent silver. You can curve and bend the clay after it had dried, which means it is ideal for creating braids, knots and curved pieces.

PMC Sterling contains 7.5 per cent copper and 92.5 per cent silver. This makes the fired pieces stronger than fired silver. However, because it contains copper, this part of the precious metal clay requires a higher firing temperature. The metal will oxidise, so it needs to be fired in two stages like copper clay.

PASTE CLAY

Paste clay has the same silver content as lump clay but is a watered down version; paste clay is used in the same way as slip would be in ceramic clay making. Paste clay can stick two pieces of unfired clay together and be used as a decorative effect on the surface of lump clay. It can also be painted in layers onto organic objects such as feathers, flowers and leaves. When the clay has dried and it is fired, the organic matter will burn away, leaving a beautiful silver replica in its place. If you do not have any paste clay, you can make your own by adding water to lump clay or grinding down pieces of dried clay and adding a few drops of water.

At the time of writing, Aida Industries recently launched a new paste clay product that has a much stronger formula. This new paste clay can be used to attach two pieces of fired silver clay together. The new formula now contains 90 per cent silver and 10 per cent binder, whereas the previous paste type contained 80 per cent silver and 20 per cent binder.

SYRINGE CLAY

Syringe clay has a slightly stiffer consistency than paste clay and is contained within a syringe with a nozzle at the end. The syringe allows you to dispense the clay in a more controlled way than paste clay. This means that as well as using syringe clay to stick pieces together and fill gaps and cracks, you can create decorative effects by extruding the clay through the syringe onto specific areas of your work.

Copper and bronze clay

Copper was one of the earliest metals discovered by man and as such is one of the oldest metals in use for jewellery making. Bronze is a stronger metal, however, because it is an alloy of copper and tin. Its original purpose was for making articles that needed great strength, such as weapons, tools and armour. But it didn't take long for our ancient ancestors to start using it to decorate items such as sculptures, accessories and jewellery.

Copper and bronze clays were invented by American artist and metallurgist Bill Struve. He discovered a process for recycling copper and combining it with water and a non-toxic binding ingredient. The challenge was to find a way of firing it while preventing firescale from forming on the surface. When copper and bronze are heated they react with the oxygen and moisture in the air, which causes the metal to oxidise. Struve experimented and found that burying the pieces of copper and bronze clay in coconut-activated carbon inside a metal box largely eradicated the oxidisation. This breakthrough led to the development of the rapid, low-fire clays that are available today.

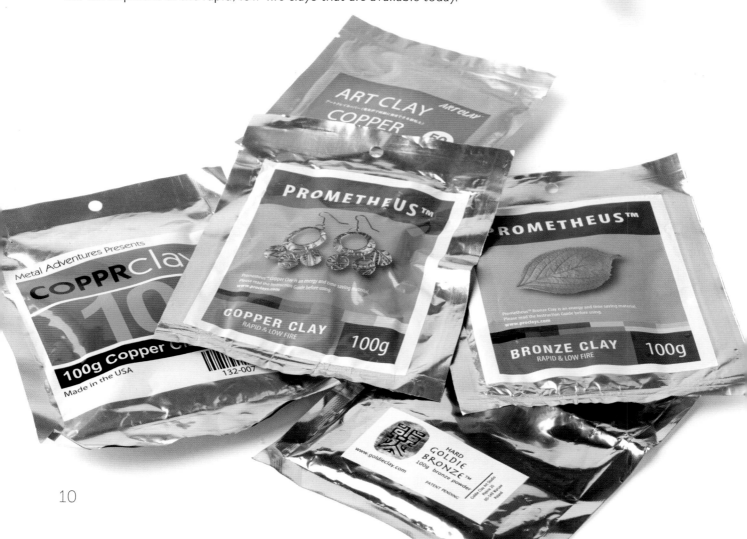

COPPER CLAY

Many of the copper clay products on the market today are known as rapid, low-fire clays. This means that they can be fired at lower temperatures (around 900°C/1652°F) and require less time for firing, usually anywhere between thirty minutes and three hours, depending on the size and thickness of the piece.

All of the copper clay pieces in this book have been created using Art Clay Copper. Guideline firing temperatures and times for each of the copper pieces in this book can be found on pages 168–169. If you are using a different brand of copper clay, please refer to the manufacturer's recommended firing instructions.

The best way to fire copper clay is in a kiln. The pieces are fired in two stages and at the second stage of firing they are buried in coconut-activated carbon within a metal box. This removes a great deal of the opportunity for firescale to occur because there is no moisture, and very little oxygen can reach the piece beneath the charcoal. Copper clay pieces no bigger than 4cm (1½in) and no thicker than seven playing cards thick can be fired with a gas torch.

BRONZE CLAY

Bronze clay is made up of 90 per cent copper and ten per cent tin, but this ten per cent makes a big difference to the appearance of bronze clay after firing; the tin gives it an almost golden finish. It has a slightly duller finish than fired copper clay, but it is equally beautiful and gives further scope for jewellery design.

I have used Prometheus Bronze Clay for the bronze projects in this book, but there is a range of other bronze clays available, such as Goldie Bronze and Hadar's Clay. These bronze clays come in powder form, which you mix with water to form lump clay. They are simple to use and have a similar firing schedule to Prometheus Bronze Clay. The benefit of using powdered clay is that you can mix up just the right amount for each project and store the powder until you need to use it again. All the instructions for firing the bronze pieces can be found on pages 168–169.

11

Basic equipment

There is certain equipment that you will use time and time again, regardless of the type of metal clay you're using. Here are some of my must-have items.

PLASTIC FOOD WRAP

This is a necessity when working with metal clays: you can knead the clay while it is covered in plastic wrap – to condition it and prevent it sticking to your hands – and it can be used to prevent excess clay drying out. Store the plastic-wrapped clay inside a screw-top jar or airtight container along with a damp baby wipe to create a moist atmosphere, so that the clay remains hydrated between uses.

MODELLING CLAY

I would advise you to first create a version of your design using modelling or polymer clay before you commit to using metal clay – this will enable you to see how the design looks, work out how much metal clay you need and practise the techniques.

CLAY BALM

At the start of each project it is essential to apply a thin layer of clay balm to your rolling pin and rolling surface – I like to use a square of teflon – as well as any cutters and texture mats you will be using. Select a balm that is formulated for use with metal clays – these products tend to contain ingredients such as natural oils, beeswax and cocoa butter. Alternatively, olive oil is perfect for using as a resist on your work surface and hands. Avoid using petroleum-based balms as they can react adversely with the binding agents in the clays.

TEXTURE STAMPS

One of the greatest advantages metal clays have over sheet metal is that you can easily add texture and pattern to them. A huge number of rubber and plastic texture sheets are made especially for metal clays.

BABY WIPES

These are ideal for cleaning the metal residue from your hands, tools and work surfaces as you work. They are also very useful for helping to refine dried clay. Rub a damp baby wipe along the edges of your dried clay pieces to give a smooth, silky finish to the clay.

HOLE-MAKING TOOLS

Sooner or later you will need to cut holes in your metal clay, either for attaching findings or for decoration. It is easiest to do this before firing, when the clay is either wet or dried. You can use everyday items such as drinking straws and cocktail sticks while the clay is wet; a pin vice is ideal for use on dried, unfired clay; while a drill can be used for fired metal clay.

ROLLING TOOLS

I use two rolling tools. The first is a mini rolling pin, or mini roller, which allows you to roll clay to even thicknesses. The second is a snake roller – a small clear rectangle of perspex, which will help you roll perfectly even ropes of clay (see page 42).

PLAYING CARDS

Playing cards will help you to keep your clay level and at a specific thickness when you roll it out. Place the required number of cards on either side of your clay and keep the ends of the rolling pin on top of the cards as you roll. This will ensure that the clay does not become thinner than the depth of the cards. One playing card is equivalent to 1mm ($^1/_{25}$ in); tape the cards together to prevent them from moving around. There are alternatives, such as plastic slats of varying thicknesses and clay rolling frames.

CUTTING TOOLS

You can buy cutters in a wide assortment of shapes and sizes –
think creatively when you source them: cookie cutters or sugarcraft
cutters can be ideal. For geometric shapes you will need a tissue
blade – a straight, fine blade – and for more complex templates a
fine needle tool or craft pick is essential for freehand cutting.

SANDING MATERIALS

The more neatly you finish your pieces before firing the better they will look afterwards. Remember also that it is much easier to sand and smooth dry clay than it is to file fired metals. You will need to use different grades of sanding sponge and polishing papers to smooth and refine your pieces before firing. Start with the coarsest grade, working your way to the finest.

PAINTBRUSH

You will need a paintbrush for sealing joins, applying paste, smoothing any imperfections and for working with ropes of clay. It is worth having a variety of sizes, to suit the size of the piece you are working on. Always clean your paintbrushes thoroughly after use.

METAL POLISH

Metal polish will create a mirror-like finish on fired pieces of metal clay. Use a cloth or paper towel to apply a small amount, then use a soft cloth to clean the polish away and to buff the surface of the metal.

WIRE BRUSH

Immediately after firing, your pieces of metal clay will have a dull finish – you will need to use a wire brush to remove the surface layer and reveal the beautiful shine of the metal. It is worth investing in a brass or fine wire brush for each type of metal clay you use, keeping the brushes separate so that you don't cross-contaminate the different metals.

AGATE BURNISHER

Use this to burnish the surface of the metal clay to flatten it and create a high shine. It is particularly effective for polishing the edges of pieces and any piece that has a close texture. It is not recommended for plain pieces or for use on large, flat areas of metal because it can scratch the surface.

Jewellery-making tools

These are essential jewellery-making tools, and I have used them in virtually every project.

FLAT-NOSE PLIERS

These are used to bend sharp corners in wire and for holding things flat, straightening wire and opening and closing jump rings. They are available in a variety of sizes.

ROUND-NOSE PLIERS

Use these to make loops and coils in wire, head pins and eye pins.

CRIMPING PLIERS

Use these to press crimps together to secure the end of beading thread (see page 37).

SIDE CUTTERS

This handy tool is essential for cutting beading thread and wire and for trimming excess wire from head pins, eye pins and rivets.

BEZELLING TOOLS

A bezel rocker and curved burnisher are used to set gemstones in bezel wire after firing.

HAMMERS

A raw hide mallet is used to flatten or to reshape pieces after firing; a jeweller's hammer is used for riveting and flattening wire; both are useful additions to your kit.

TWEEZERS

These are useful when setting stones, picking up hot pieces and for other fine detail work.

RING-MAKING TOOLS

A ring gauge and ring-sizing papers for measuring precise ring sizes are both very useful tools. You will also need a wooden ring mandrel to place your clay ring on as it dries.

Firing tools

Most important of all is the firing equipment. There is some equipment that you will need for any method of firing, such as protective goggles, long tweezers or tongs, and a metal tray or heat-resistant container of water for quenching hot pieces of metal. But there are three ways you can fire your pieces, and this is what you will need for each:

FOR GAS STOVE FIRING:

- Gas stove
- Piece of heat-proof wire mesh

FOR GAS TORCH FIRING:

- Jewellers' gas torch: use a small torch for firing silver clay because this can be fired at a temperature of 650–800°C (1202–1472°F). Use a larger, hotter torch for firing copper and bronze clay because these metals need to be fired at a temperature of 820°C (1508°F) for bronze clay, and 900°C (1652°F) for copper clay
- Butane-propane gas mixture
- Firing block

FOR KILN FIRING:

- Kiln: you will need a kiln that reaches the following minimum temperatures: 650°C (1202°F) for silver clay; 820°C (1508°F) for bronze clay; 900°C (1652°F) for copper clay
- Fibre blanket to support your pieces during firing
- Steel box with lid, for copper and bronze pieces
- Coconut-activated carbon or magic carbon, for copper and bronze pieces

Pickling equipment

After firing, you will need to place your copper and bronze pieces in a pickle solution to remove any firescale (see page 35). A small slow cooker is the ideal receptacle for pickling your metal clay pieces. It will maintain a gentle heat and has a lid to prevent the solution from evaporating. You could also place the pickle solution in a lidded thermal cup flask, or use a saucepan to gently heat the pickle solution. Be sure to place a lid over it and keep it at a very low heat. Do not then use these receptacles for food.

17

Turning your metal clay into jewellery

For me, the most exciting part of jewellery making is selecting the materials, settings and findings to complement my metal clay designs in just the right way. As well as the essentials that enable your creations to be worn, such as jump rings, chain and earring wires, here are some other important materials to consider.

GEMSTONES AND BEADS

I love to use a variety of different gemstones and beads in my designs. In the projects in this book I have mainly used them as embellishments, but you could also use beads to string necklaces and bracelets. I like to combine genuine gemstones with my precious metal designs, and these days natural gemstones have become much more affordable, so adding a beautiful, high-quality element to your jewellery need not break the bank.

CHAIN

It is important to choose the style of chain that fits best with your design. Sterling silver chain looks beautiful used with creations made from silver clay, while copper and bronze pieces look wonderful with vintage chain. Sometimes a fashion chain with large or unusually shaped links will be the perfect finishing touch (see the mouse charms project, pages 50–55). Raid your jewellery box and browse charity shops for old pieces of jewellery from which you can upcycle chain.

FINDINGS

These are the crucial components that will transform your metal clay, chain and beads into jewellery. Findings include jump rings (small rings that connect components together), earring wires, clasps, head pins, eye pins, crimps and crimp covers. Consider whether you want to use sterling silver or plated findings, or choose from a range of metal colours including silver, copper, gold, rose gold and antique bronze.

THREADING MATERIALS

If you are threading beads to form a necklace or bracelet, you will need beading thread (also known as tiger tail). Different gauges of wire are also useful during jewellery making, for example for setting pearls on page 134. You can also use wire to create bails on fired pieces and to attach other components or materials to your metal pieces.

OTHER MATERIALS

Leather in different colours and textures makes a wonderful addition to these jewellery pieces. It gives them a modern but very high-end look. See pages 88, 152 and 163 for more inspiration.

Suede and nylon cords in every colour are the perfect adjustable stringing materials for creating necklaces, and give a contemporary look. See pages 71 and 80. Resin is ideal for adding a protective glossy coating to your pieces and for injecting colour. See page 113.

Techniques

This section contains all the basic techniques you need for working with metal clays. We will look at how to get started; how to handle and store your clay once you have opened the packet; drying your pieces; reconstituting excess dried-out clay; and – most importantly – how to fire your pieces, whether they be silver, copper or bronze.

Silver clay

Of all the metal clays, silver is the easiest to handle and the simplest and quickest to fire. It has a relatively long working time and is easy to rehydrate. I would always advise anyone who is new to metal clays to start with silver clay. The following techniques form the basis of many of the projects and will help you achieve great results every time.

PREPARING

1 Gather together all the tools and materials you will need before you open your packet of clay. Ensure that all of your equipment has been cleaned thoroughly to remove all traces of other metal clays to avoid contamination. Use a baby wipe or damp cloth to clean them if need be.

2 Remove as much silver clay as you need from its packaging and place it inside some plastic wrap. Knead the clay for a minute or two to soften it and make it malleable, ready for use.

HANDLING

Rubbing a little clay balm or olive oil onto your hands when handling the clay will prevent it from sticking to your fingers. If the clay dries out while you are working with it, simply add a drop or two of water, place it in some plastic wrap and knead the clay to bring it back to a soft and workable state.

ROLLING

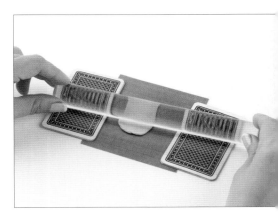

1 Each project's instructions will tell you how thick the clay needs to be: tape together two sets of playing cards of the corresponding thickness. For a standard piece, a thickness of five playing cards will give a good strong finish when fired.

2 Add a thin layer of clay balm to your work surface and rolling pin. Place a set of playing cards on each side of your work surface.

3 Roll out the silver clay between the playing cards, turning the clay occasionally, until you have achieved the shape you want. The playing cards will ensure that the clay is an even depth all over and will prevent you from rolling it too thinly.

KEEPING CLAY MOIST

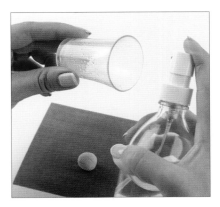

This is a simple way to keep your clay moist while you are working with it. Take a plastic shot glass and glue a piece of sponge into the base. Mist the sponge and the inside of the shot glass with water from a spray bottle. Place the shot glass over your clay. This keeps the clay perfectly hydrated as you work.

STORING UNUSED CLAY

Once it is out of the packet, silver clay must be stored in moist conditions or it will dry out. Tightly wrap any unused clay in plastic wrap and place inside a screwtop jar or airtight container. Add a damp baby wipe or a wet piece of cloth to the container – this will create a moist environment and ensure that the clay stays hydrated.

Unopened packets of silver clay have a shelf life of up to five years. Store unopened packets in a cool, dark place. Do not refrigerate or freeze them.

Bronze and copper clay

Bronze and copper clays perform in very similar ways: copper clay is 99.9 per cent copper after firing and bronze clay contains 90 per cent copper and 10 per cent tin. Prometheus copper clay has a fairly crumbly consistency so needs to be conditioned well before using. Art Clay copper and Prometheus bronze clay are beautifully soft and can be used straight from the packet.

top tip

Bronze and copper clay pieces fired with a small gas torch (up to 900°C/1652°F) should be no larger than 3cm (1¼in) and no thicker than 4mm (³/₁₆in). If you would like to torch-fire pieces larger than this you will need to use a larger, hotter torch (up to 1500°C/2732°F). If you are firing your pieces in a kiln then you can make a piece any size you wish, provided it will fit inside your kiln space.

PREPARING

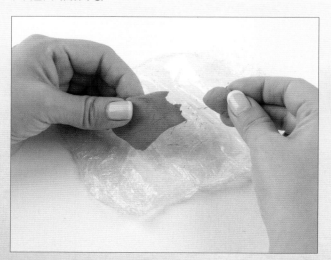

All your tools and equipment must be cleaned thoroughly to remove all traces of other metal clays. Use a baby wipe or damp cloth to clean them off. When you are ready to start creating your design, only take as much clay out of the packet as you need to work with, especially if you are using bronze, as it will begin to oxidise and discolour if it stays out in the open air.

ROLLING

To prevent the clay sticking, add a thin layer of clay balm or olive oil to your work surface and rolling pin. When you have chosen your thickness, place the requisite number of playing cards on either side of your clay. The playing cards will keep the clay an even depth as you roll, and prevent you from rolling too thinly.

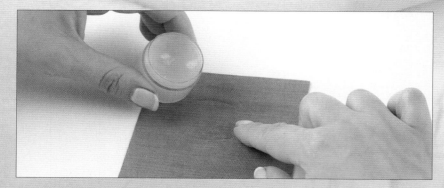

HANDLING

I would advise you to apply a barrier cream to your hands before handling bronze or copper clay. The binding ingredients in the clay are non-toxic, but the clay itself can occasionally irritate and stain the skin. Wash your hands or at least clean them with a baby wipe after handling the clay to avoid ingesting the metal particles and to avoid staining your skin and fingernails. You may wish to wear latex gloves.

STORING UNUSED CLAY

Wrap unused pieces of bronze and copper clay in plastic wrap and place inside a screwtop jar or airtight container. Add a damp baby wipe or a wet piece of cloth to the container – this will create a moist environment and keep the clay hydrated.

Metal clay that remains unopened in its packaging has a shelf life of up to five years so there is no rush to use it up. Store unopened packs in a cool, dark place. Do not refrigerate or freeze.

CONDITIONING

Bronze and copper clays are not as naturally silky as silver clay, and may need softening up if they have dried out in storage. To condition them, add a few drops of liquid glycerine or water and knead for a few minutes inside a piece of plastic wrap. The texture of the clay needs to be smooth and supple; if, after kneading, it is still cracked or lumpy, you may need to add a little more water or glycerine and knead for a little longer.

2

1

Drying metal clay

You must allow your pieces of metal clay to dry out completely before you fire them. If there is any moisture left inside the piece when it is fired it will cause the metal to crack or blister – as the metal heats up the moisture will work its way towards the surface as it tries to escape. To check if the clay is completely dry, put the hot clay (straight from drying) on a cold mirror. After 10–20 seconds, move it and check that no condensation has formed on the mirror. This test is especially important for large and thick pieces of jewellery. If you are in any doubt as to whether a piece has dried out for long enough, err on the side of caution – be patient and fire it at a later stage.

The table on the facing page gives guideline drying times for metal clays based on a test piece weighing 5g ($^1/_5$ oz). The hair dryer referred to in the chart is 1200w, held 3–5cm (1¼–1¾in) away from the piece of metal clay. These are the minimum recommended drying times. Extend the drying time if a larger amount of clay is used or if any additional liquid has been added to the clay.

top tip

There are no limits to how long you can leave a piece of metal clay to dry, or how long you can keep it once dried. Simply store the piece at room temperature in a dry place where it won't get knocked or damaged, until you are ready to fire it.

DRYING WITH HEAT

A hot plate, such as the one shown here, is an excellent way to dry your pieces in a relatively short amount of time. Be careful when handling them once they have dried, as the clay surface will get very hot. Alternatively, use a hair dryer to dry your pieces.

top tip

If you don't own a hot plate or dehydrator, there are a number of different options to speed up the drying process. Place your clay pieces on a teflon sheet on a baking tray and put them into a cool oven. Keep the temperature no higher than 80°C (176°F) because you do not want the binder to burn away. You can also place the pieces inside an airing cupboard or on top of a radiator – anywhere that is warm and dry.

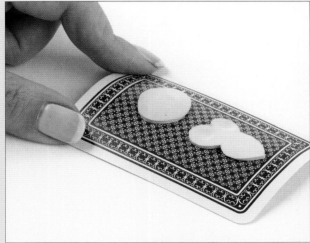

DRYING AT ROOM TEMPERATURE

The easiest drying method, but the one that takes the longest, is to leave your pieces to dry naturally at room temperature – just make sure you put them somewhere they won't get damaged, either on a piece of greaseproof paper or on your teflon working surface.

DRYING IN SHAPE

If you want pieces of clay to dry in a particular three-dimensional shape, support them in that position as they are drying. I use door knobs and light bulbs for pieces that need a domed shape, or playing cards that have been flexed into position to give a curve. Always remember to apply some balm to the supporting surface to prevent the clay from sticking to it.

METAL CLAY PRODUCT	ROOM TEMPERATURE	HAIR DRYER	HOT PLATE, OVEN, KILN OR FOOD DEHYDRATOR
ART CLAY SILVER 650	24 hours	15 minutes	10 minutes at 150°C (302°F)
PMC+	24 hours	15–30 minutes	15–30 minutes at 150°C (302°F)
PMC 3	24 hours	15–30 minutes	15–30 minutes at 150°C (302°F)
PROMETHEUS BRONZE	24 hours	20–30 minutes	1 hour at 150°C (302°F)
PROMETHEUS COPPER	24 hours	20–30 minutes	1 hour at 150°C (302°F)
ART CLAY COPPER	24 hours	20–30 minutes	1 hour at 150°C (302°F)

Reconstituting metal clay

Metal clays can dry out quite quickly while you are working with them or when they are not in use. While there is nothing quite as good as clay that is brand new, it is possible to bring dried or cracked clay back to a workable state. So select which option applies to you and follow these troubleshooting tips.

IF YOUR CLAY HAS DRIED OUT COMPLETELY

If your clay pieces have dried out completely, or you made a design that you no longer want to fire, it is possible to reconstitute the dried pieces back into lump clay by grinding them up and rehydrating them.

1 Place the pieces of dried-out clay in a mortar. Use a pestle to grind the clay into a fine powder.

2 Wrap a piece of hosiery tightly over a small container (7–10 denier stockings work well for this purpose).

3 Place the ground clay powder on top of the hosiery, which will act like a sieve. Use a small brush to push the powder through into the container.

4 The powder will pass easily through and any lumps of clay will remain on the top. Return the lumps of clay to the mortar and grind them again. Repeat steps 1–3 as necessary until all the clay passes through.

5 Remove the hosiery and add some water to the clay powder a drop at a time.

6 Use a palette knife to bind the powder and water together and reconstitute the mixture back into lump clay. If the clay becomes too sticky, allow it to air dry for a few minutes before kneading and re-using.

IF YOUR CLAY HAS A CRACKED APPEARANCE

If your clay has begun to dry out and takes on a cracked appearance while you are working with it, simply add a couple of drops of water, place it in some plastic wrap and knead it for a few minutes to work the moisture back into the clay. You may want to use a few drops of liquid glycerine with copper and bronze clay, instead of water.

IF STORED CLAY IS TOO DRY TO WORK WITH

If excess clay you have stored has become too dry to work with, poke a few holes in the surface of the clay, then cut it into smaller chunks. Add a little water and knead the clay pieces. Place the clay in a screwtop jar or airtight container along with a damp baby wipe or piece of wet cloth. Ensure that the clay and cloth or baby wipe are not touching. Leave the clay to rehydrate for 24 hours then knead it back into a workable state. If the clay has become wet or sticky, allow it to air dry for a few minutes before use.

Firing silver clay

When metal clays are fired to the correct temperature, the binding ingredient burns away and the metal particles melt together. This process is known as sintering. Silver clay has the simplest and quickest firing process of all the metal clays; small pieces can be fired in as little time as two minutes (see pages 168–169 for firing times and temperatures). Silver clay can be fired in three ways: with a gas torch, on a gas stove or in a kiln.

warning!

Do not fire metal pieces that contain pieces of glass or ceramics with a gas torch because the instant intensity of heat will crack or shatter them.

FIRING WITH A GAS TORCH

This is the quickest method of firing so don't be put off by the idea of working with a live flame. This method puts you in control of directing the heat, so you need to stay alert and be careful not to overheat and melt the silver. Art Clay Silver 650, PMC+ and PMC 3 silver clay products can be fired with a gas torch. This method is best for pieces weighing up to 25g (1oz) and no larger than 5 x 5 x 2cm (2 x 2 x ¾in). Cubic zirconia and certain gemstones up to 5mm (¼in) are safe to be fired using this method.

warning!

Tie long hair back and ensure you have no articles of clothing that could come into contact with the flame. Wear a pair of safety goggles.

1 Place the dried silver clay piece on the centre of a fire-resistant block. Ensure you have all your safety equipment to hand, as well as a heat-resistant bowl full of water for quenching.

2 Turn on the gas torch and direct the flame towards the metal clay at a 45-degree angle. Hold the torch at a distance of around 5cm (2in).

top tip

If the piece begins to shimmer or looks glossy this means it has become too hot and is beginning to melt. Direct the flame away from the piece for a few seconds, then slowly bring it back towards the piece until it glows a peach colour once more.

3 Slowly move the flame over the piece to heat it evenly. A little smoke and flame will be released as the binder burns away. When the piece begins to glow a peach colour, start to time the firing. If possible, ask someone else to turn the lights off in the room so that you can see the colour of the hot metal. Heat for the recommended length of time (according to the instructions on pages 168–169).

4 Either allow the piece to cool naturally on your firing block or use tweezers or tongs to pick up the piece and quench it in cold water. Never quench pieces that contain glass, gemstones, cubic zirconia or ceramics – as the swift change in temperature can cause them to shatter – instead allow these to cool naturally.

5 Your fired metal will be left with a white coating. Brush the piece with a wire brush to remove this coating and reveal the shiny metal below.

FIRING ON A GAS STOVE

This method is ideal for silver clay pieces weighing up to 30g (1oz) and no larger than 5 x 5 x 2cm (2 x 2 x ¾in). Projects that contain gemstones no larger than 5mm (¼in) can also be fired this way. Pieces containing glass or ceramics should not be fired on a gas stove.

1 Place a piece of stainless steel mesh onto your gas stove. Turn the stove on and light the gas.

2 Place your dried silver clay piece on the mesh where it is glowing brightest. You will see a flame and some smoke as the binder burns away.

3 Wait until the silver clay piece glows peach – the colour it turns when at optimum heat – then set a timer.

4 Once the firing time is complete, turn off the gas and allow the piece to cool before handling. Alternatively, use some metal tongs to pick up the piece and quench it in a heat-resistant bowl of cold water. Do not quench pieces that contain gemstones or cubic zirconia – allow these to cool down naturally.

top tip

Turn off the room lights during firing so that you can see the colour of the silver clay piece clearly.

KILN FIRING

If you want to fire bigger pieces with no restrictions on the weight of the clay, or if you want to make projects containing large quantities of organic materials, or that contain glass or ceramics, a kiln is the best option.

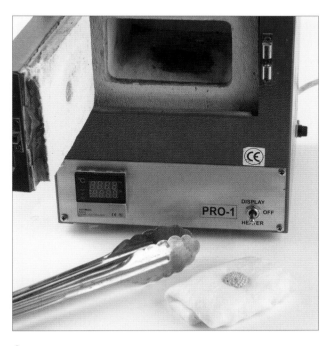

1 Place the dried silver clay piece on a kiln shelf or piece of fibre blanket. For large, complex pieces, pack the fibre blanket underneath the clay, to support the piece and prevent it from warping. Use long-handled metal tongs to place it inside the kiln.

2 Close the door and set the kiln to the required temperature – see pages 168–169 for firing temperatures and times. Do not start to time the firing until the kiln has reached the required temperature. After the firing time has been reached, turn off the kiln.

top tip

As an alternative to step 2, you can pre-heat the kiln to the required temperature and then place your pieces inside, starting the timer once the kiln regains the desired temperature.

3 Either allow the pieces to cool inside the kiln by opening the door and leaving it ajar, or remove the shelf or fibre blanket from the kiln using metal tongs and place the piece on a heat-resistant surface. If you don't want to wait for the silver to cool naturally, you can quench it in cold water (see step 4, facing page). Do not quench pieces containing glass, gemstones, cubic zirconia or ceramics.

Firing bronze and copper clay

Bronze and copper clays are fired at a higher temperature than silver clay (see pages 168–169 for firing times and temperatures). This means that gas stove firing alone is not an option as it does not produce high enough temperatures. The additional challenge when firing copper and bronze clays is to try to minimise oxidisation. If the metal oxidises, a reddish-brown crust known as firescale appears on the piece. It can be removed using a pickle solution (see page 35), but the aim is to prevent it from forming in the first place. Follow these steps to ensure your bronze and copper clay pieces are fully sintered with minimal firescale.

FIRING WITH A GAS TORCH

The method for firing both bronze and copper metal clays by gas torch is exactly the same. Use this method for firing pieces that are smaller than 3cm x 3cm x 5mm (1¼ x 1¼ x ¼in). Pieces containing cubic zirconia, gemstones, glass or ceramics should not be fired with a gas torch.

1 Place the dried copper or bronze clay piece on the centre of a fire-resistant block. Place a large heat-resistant container full of cold water next to the firing block.

2 Ignite the gas torch and direct the flame towards the metal clay piece at a 45-degree angle. Hold the torch at a distance of about 5cm (2in).

warning!
Tie long hair back and ensure you have no articles of clothing that could come into contact with the flame. Wear a pair of safety goggles.

3 Slowly move the flame over the piece to heat it evenly. A little smoke and flame will be released as the binder burns away. Concentrate the heat on the piece until it turns a bright orange-red colour. At this point you can start to time the firing. If possible, ask someone else to turn the lights off so that you can clearly see the colour of the hot metal. Heat for the recommended length of time (according to the instructions on pages 168–169).

top tip

It is quite difficult to overheat or melt copper and bronze clay pieces because they need to reach continuous temperatures of 900°C (1652°F) for copper clay, and 820°C (1508°F) for bronze clay. Instead, your biggest concern is likely to be ensuring the pieces reach a hot enough temperature for a long enough time to become fully sintered.

5 Pickle your fired pieces to remove any firescale – follow the instructions on page 35.

4 As soon as the firing time is completed, pick up the piece using a long pair of tongs and quench it in cold water. Do not wait for the piece to cool naturally because the moment the heat is no longer concentrated on the metal it will begin to oxidise. Quenching immediately helps to prevent the piece developing firescale.

KILN FIRING GUIDE

A kiln allows you to fire large pieces of copper or bronze clay with no restrictions on the weight. I find that the following method is the safest and most effective way of kiln firing Art Clay copper, Prometheus copper and bronze clay and Goldie bronze clay.

top tip

You can fire a mix of copper and bronze pieces at the same time: heat the kiln to 820°C (1508°F) and fire for two hours.

1 The first stage of the process requires you to fire the dried piece either on a gas stove or in a kiln at 350°C (662°F) for about ten minutes. See page 168 for further information. My preferred method is gas stove firing: place the piece, or pieces, on a piece of stainless steel mesh on top of a gas stove. Fire for ten minutes, then allow to cool down.

2 Put approximately 3cm (1¼in) of coconut-activated carbon in the bottom of a steel box.

3 Place your clay piece on top of the coconut-activated carbon – if you are firing more than one piece, position them so that there is at least 1.5cm (½in) space between them. Cover the piece with coconut-activated carbon, then put the lid on.

4 Place the box in the preheated kiln: 820°C (1508°F) for Prometheus bronze clay and Goldie bronze clay, and 900°C (1652°F) for Art Clay copper and Prometheus copper clay. Allow the kiln to reach the temperature again and set your timer for 60 minutes. When the firing is complete, either leave the pieces to cool down in the kiln with the door ajar, or carefully take out the box and leave it on a heat-resistant surface until it is cool enough to remove the pieces. Pickle them following the instructions on the facing page.

PICKLING COPPER AND BRONZE CLAY

Pickling is the process of removing impurities from metal using a warm acidic solution; it will remove firescale from oxidised pieces of fired bronze or copper clay. Some pieces will take longer to pickle than others, depending on the amount of firescale. Modern pickling solutions contain fruit acids, so they are safe to use and not harmful to the skin. I use a slow cooker to heat my pickle solution, but you could use a saucepan.

top tip

Follow the manufacturer's instructions carefully – different types of pickle will contain varying ingredients and have their own safety precautions for disposal after use.

1 Add some pickle powder to cold water – follow the manufacturer's instructions for guidance on quantities. Put the lid on, and heat the solution until it is hot, but not boiling.

2 Place the metal into the solution using long-handled tongs and re-cover. Leave the piece to pickle for between five and thirty minutes.

3 Lift the metal out of the pickle. If oxidation remains, return it to the pickle solution and check it every minute until it is clean.

4 Rinse the piece in cold water to remove the pickle solution.

5 Brush the piece with a wire brush to reveal the metal and remove any remaining pickle.

6 Your pickled and polished piece will have a beautiful shine.

Basic jewellery techniques

HOW TO OPEN AND CLOSE A JUMP RING

1 Using two pairs of pliers, grip the jump ring on either side of the gap. Move one side towards you and the other away from you to open the jump ring. Do not pull the ring apart because it may distort the shape.

2 Insert an earring wire, chain, clasp or another jump ring.

3 To close the jump ring, grip both ends with your pliers. Bend them back together again, wiggling the ends back and forth until you feel them sliding against one another. Your jump ring ends should be perfectly aligned.

HOW TO WRAP A WIRE LOOP

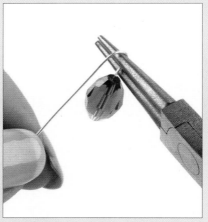

1 Thread your chosen bead onto a head pin. Using your round-nose pliers, grip the head pin approximately 4mm (³/₁₆in) above the bead. Bend the head pin to a right angle, as shown.

2 Bend the tail of the head pin around the top jaw of your pliers to form a complete loop. You may have to reposition your pliers to do this.

3 Grip the loop with your flat-nose pliers. Wrap the wire around the neck of the loop until it touches the bead. Trim the excess wire as close to the wrap as possible using side cutters.

STRINGING A BEADED NECKLACE OR BRACELET

2 Thread a crimp onto one end of the beading thread.

1 Thread the required number of beads onto a length of beading thread. Trim the thread to leave at least 10cm (4in) of excess at either end.

3 Next thread on the jump ring of the clasp.

4 Take the end of the beading thread back through the crimp and pull it to tighten the loop of thread around the jump ring of the clasp.

5 Press the crimp together using crimping pliers or flat-nose pliers.

6 Trim off the excess thread using wire cutters, or push it through as many beads as possible, then trim. Repeat this process at the other end of the beading thread, using the other half of the clasp.

MAKING A LOOP IN WIRE

1 Thread your chosen bead onto a head pin or eye pin.

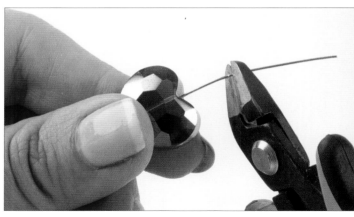

2 Trim the wire above the bead to about 1cm (½in).

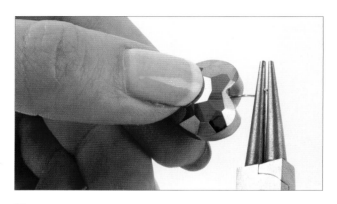

3 Hold the end of the wire with round-nose pliers and bend the wire over to form a semi-circle.

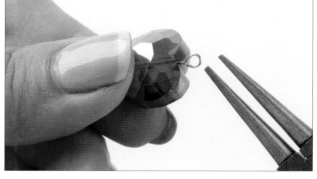

4 Let go of the wire, move the pliers around the loop a little, then continue to roll the wire until you have formed a circular loop centred above the bead.

5 Open the loop away from you, as if you were opening a door, using your flat-nose pliers.

6 Attach the loop to your finding or piece of jewellery then use your flat-nose pliers to bend the loop back into place to close it.

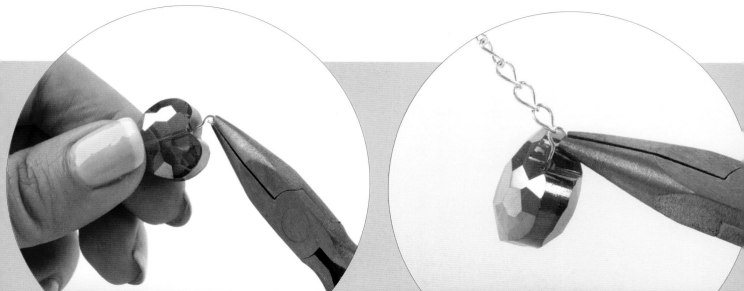

ENCLOSING CORD ENDS

1 Place the end of the cord inside the opening of the cord end finding.

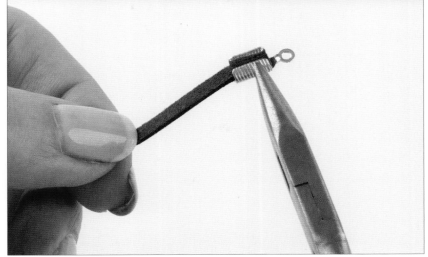

2 Take a pair of chain-nose pliers and press down one of the metal flaps of the finding onto the cord.

3 Press the second flap down with the pliers. Press the two flaps down very firmly with the pliers to ensure the cord is securely contained inside the metal.

4 Open a jump ring and attach it to the hole in the cord end finding. Attach the open jump ring to the loop at the base of the lobster claw clasp.

5 Close the jump ring securely using two pairs of chain-nose pliers.

6 Repeat steps 1 and 2 to attach the second cord end finding to the opposite end of the cord. Attach a jump ring to the hole in the other cord end finding. Close the jump ring with two pairs of chain-nose pliers.

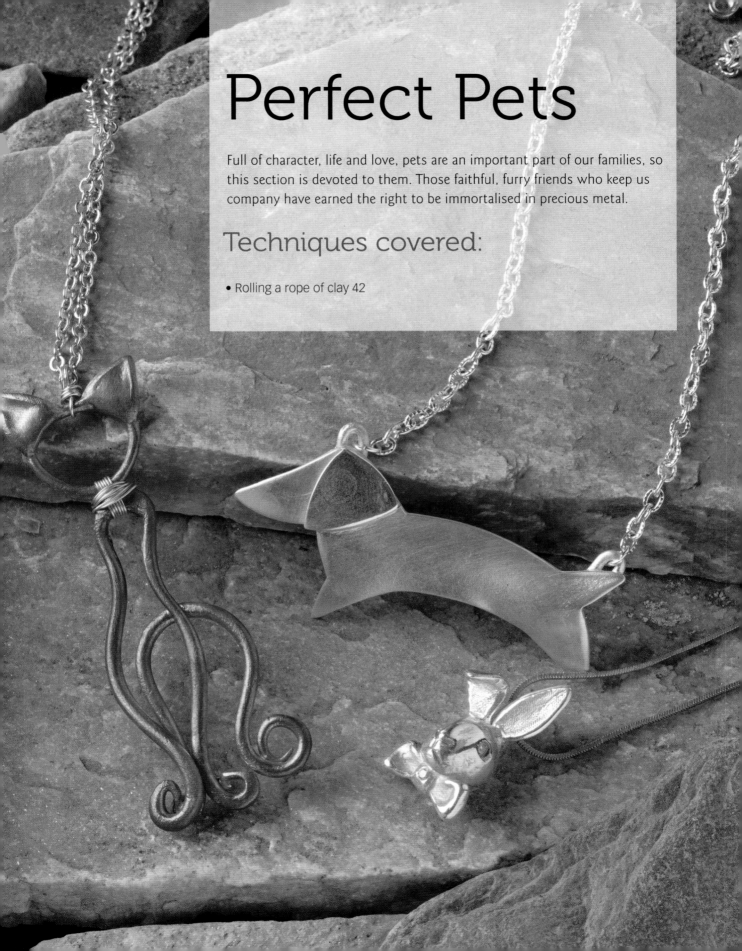

Perfect Pets

Full of character, life and love, pets are an important part of our families, so this section is devoted to them. Those faithful, furry friends who keep us company have earned the right to be immortalised in precious metal.

Techniques covered:

Cat pendant

So many people love fabulous felines, including me. I wanted to capture my own cat's elegance and aloofness by creating a simple silhouette using ropes of clay. This is such an effective way of creating just about any animal shape you like.

Key Technique: rolling a rope of clay

Rolling clay into a rope helps it to go a very long way. You will find ropes of clay very useful for creating decorative effects or to create a larger project by connecting the ropes together. It is very important to keep the rope of clay hydrated while you are shaping it – this keeps it flexible and malleable. Use a snake roller to roll the rope of clay to the desired length and thickness. After rolling, wet the rope generously with water. Allow the water to be absorbed into the clay for a few seconds and then you can mould and shape the rope much more easily.

MATERIALS

25g (⁴/₅oz) copper clay
Ceramic tile or craft mat
Snake roller
Teflon sheet
Small paintbrush
Cup of water
Sponge sanding pad
Clay modelling tool
Firing equipment
Pickling equipment
Brass wire brush
20cm (8in) gold-coloured wire, 0.4mm gauge
Wire cutters
Gold-coloured chain necklace (the length of your choice)
Round-nose pliers

1 Take a quarter of the copper clay and roll it into a sausage shape. Place the clay on a ceramic tile or craft mat and roll it into a rope with a snake roller. The rope should measure about 8cm (3½in) in length.

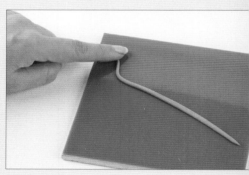

2 Roll each end of the rope with your finger to create a fine point.

3 Transfer the rope of clay onto a teflon sheet. Moisten the rope of clay with a wet paintbrush. Use the paintbrush to gently move the clay to form the shape of the cat's upper body and front legs.

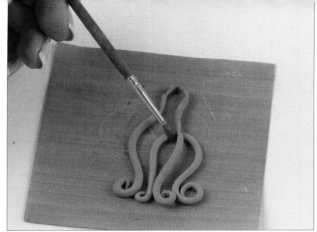

4   Using a wet paintbrush, coax the ends of the clay to form coils at each side, creating the cat's front paws. Roll another rope of clay: this rope needs to be about one-third shorter than the first rope, so use less than a quarter of the overall amount of clay. Repeat the process in steps 1–4 to create the cat's back leg, rear body and tail.

5   Allow the pieces of clay to dry according to the instructions on page 24. When the pieces have dried, mix a small piece of the copper clay with some water to create a thick paste. Apply the paste to the pieces of dried clay to stick them together as shown, to form the complete cat's body. Allow the clay to dry thoroughly.

6   Take half of the remaining copper clay and roll this into a rope measuring 8cm (3½in). Form the rope of clay into a circle and stick the ends of the clay together using a wet paintbrush. Use the wet paintbrush to form the clay circle into an oval shape. Push the clay downwards to create the shape of the cat's chin. Allow the cat's head to dry according to the instructions on page 24.

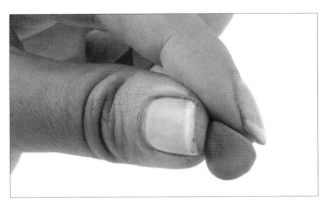

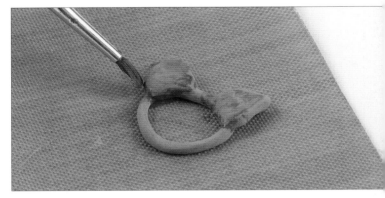

7   Take the remaining clay and cut it in half. Mould half of the clay into a triangle shape with your fingers. Pinch the clay at the top and press the centre of the shape to form the concave shape of the cat's ear. Repeat this process to make the second ear.

8   Use some copper paste to stick the ears to the head. Set the head aside to dry thoroughly again.

43

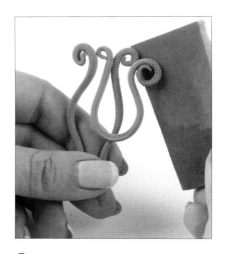

9 When the body of the cat has completely dried, use a sponge sanding pad to smooth any imperfections and to remove any excess copper paste.

10 Use the remaining copper paste to stick the cat's head to the top of the body. Apply generous amounts of paste to enable the pieces to stick securely to one another. Allow the entire cat to dry once more. When it has thoroughly dried, use the sponge sanding pad to carefully refine and smooth the entire piece before firing.

11 Fire the cat according to the instructions on pages 168–169. After firing, place the cat in a pickle solution (see page 35) to remove any firescale. Brush the cat with a brass brush to reveal the copper and to give the cat a satin finish.

12 Cut a 10cm (4in) length of gold-coloured wire. Wrap this around the head and neck of the cat to give it a decorative finish and to make the piece more secure. Trim off any excess with a pair of wire cutters.

13 To make a bail, take a 10cm (4in) length of gold-coloured wire. Pass this through the head in between the ears so that both ends of the wire meet. Use some round-nose pliers to form the wires into a loop at the top of the head. Wrap the excess wire around the loop two or three times. Trim off the excess wire with wire cutters. Thread a gold necklace chain through the bail to complete the project.

Sausage dog pendant

This project was inspired by my friend Laurie's sausage dogs. They are so adorable and I find the silhouette such a beautiful shape. This gave me the idea of creating a template of the overall shape but adding some dimension by curving the body and adding the ear in relief to the rest of the dog's face. It is a simple project to make but is a very pretty pendant. This piece can be made in whatever size you wish and would also look good as a bracelet.

MATERIALS

Templates (page 174), card and scissors

Clay balm

Teflon sheet

20g (¾oz) silver clay

Mini roller

Playing cards

Clay pick or craft knife

Sponge sanding pad

Dry polishing papers

Small paintbrush

Cup of water

Ruler

Silver syringe clay

Cocktail stick

Fibre blanket

Firing equipment

Brass wire brush

Silver polish

Polishing pad

Agate burnisher

Four silver jump rings, 6mm (¼in)

Silver necklace chain (the length of your choice)

Two pairs of pliers

Wire cutters

Silver clasp

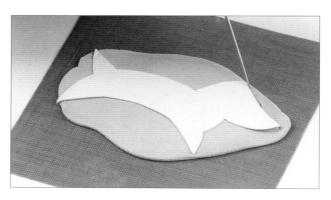

1 Draw out the templates for the sausage dog's body and ear on thin card (see page 174). Cut these pieces out. Apply a thin layer of balm to a sheet of teflon. Roll 20g (¾oz) of silver clay to a thickness of five playing cards. Place the sausage dog template onto the clay and cut around it with a clay pick or craft knife.

2 Take a playing card and apply a thin layer of clay balm to the surface.

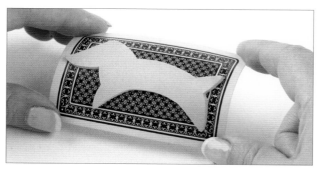

3 Bend the playing card lengthways so that it begins to curve across the middle. Place the sausage dog-shaped clay piece onto the card. Allow the clay to dry for 45 minutes on top of the curved playing card so that the clay retains its shape. After 45 minutes, gently remove the clay piece from the card and allow it dry completely.

4 Roll out the excess clay to a thickness of four playing cards and place the card template you created for the ear on top. Cut around the template with a clay pick or craft knife. Set the ear aside to dry.

5 Once the clay dog has dried completely, sand and smooth the edges, back and front of the clay with a sponge sanding pad. Use some dry polishing papers to make the surface very smooth.

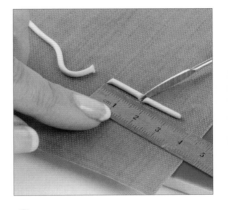

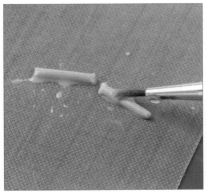

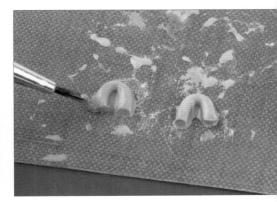

6 To make a bail for each end of the pendant, roll out a rope with the excess clay. Use a craft knife to cut two small pieces, each measuring about 1.5cm (²/₃in) long.

7 Wet each rope of clay with a small paintbrush. Allow the water to saturate the clay for a few seconds.

8 Use the paintbrush to bend each of the clay ropes into a U-shape. Set these aside to dry thoroughly.

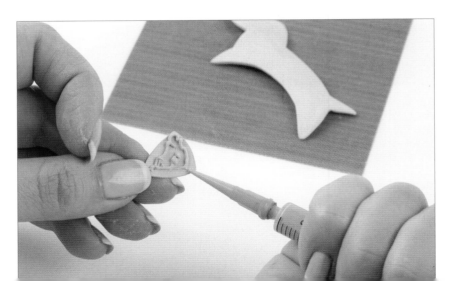

9 When the ear shape has dried completely, sand and smooth away any imperfections with a sponge sanding pad. Apply a generous amount of silver syringe clay to the back of the ear.

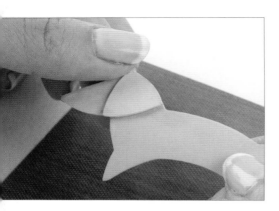
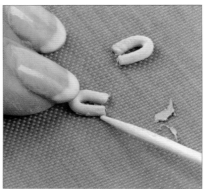
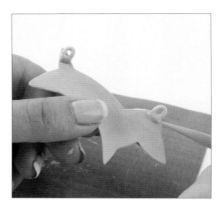

10 Press the ear shape onto the head of the clay sausage dog. Press down gently so that the ear adheres to the head. Use a damp paintbrush or a baby wipe to remove any excess clay from around the edges of the ear. Allow the piece to dry.

11 When the bails have dried out, use a cocktail stick to remove any excess pieces of clay. Gently smooth the bails with a damp baby wipe and polishing papers. Be very gentle when handling these pieces as they will be quite fragile.

12 Apply some syringe clay to the end of each bail and stick them onto the back of the dog. Place one of the bails at the top of the head and the other at the tip of the tail. Use a wet paintbrush to remove any excess clay. Allow the piece to dry fully.

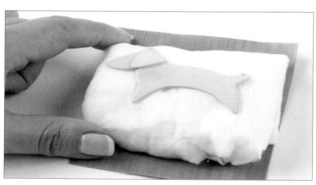

13 Do any final sanding and smoothing of the whole piece with a sponge sanding pad and polishing papers. Place the dog on a piece of fibre blanket to support the shape and to prevent it from slumping during firing. Fire according to the directions on pages 168–169.

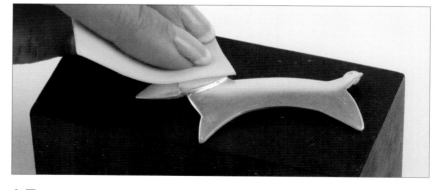

14 After the dog has been fired, allow it to cool down or quench it in cold water. Brush the piece with a brass wire brush to reveal the silver.

15 Use a polishing pad to bring a mirror-like shine to the dog's ear. Use an agate burnisher to polish the edges. Use pliers to open two jump rings and attach one to each of the bails. Cut the necklace chain in half with wire cutters. Attach one end of the chain to each jump ring and close the jump rings. Attach a jump ring to one end of the chain and attach one side of the clasp. Repeat at the other end of the chain to attach the second part of the clasp.

Mouse charms

Mice make such cute characters. They have always been a big inspiration to designers and artists, from Walt Disney to master wood craftsman Robert Thompson, who carved a little mouse into every piece he created. I decided to make these sweet and simple charms, using the mouse's tail as the bail. I have strung them on a necklace but they would also look lovely as earrings or as part of a charm bracelet.

MATERIALS

Templates (page 174), card and scissors

Clay balm

Teflon sheet

Playing cards

10g (1/3oz) of clay per mouse, whether silver, copper or bronze

Mini roller

Clay pick or craft knife

Needle file

Sponge sanding pad

Polishing papers

2.5cm (1in) fine silver wire

Round-nose pliers

Clay modelling tool

Cup of water

Pin vice with small diamond burr drill bit

Small paintbrush

Silver syringe clay

Fibre blanket

Firing equipment

Brass wire brush

Fine-line marker pen: black

Metal varnish or Renaissance wax

Acrylic necklace chain: gold-coloured

Necklace clasp: gold-coloured

Three gold-coloured jump rings, 6mm (1/4in)

Chain-nose pliers

1 Draw out the template of the mouse's head and body (see page 174) on a piece of card and cut out.

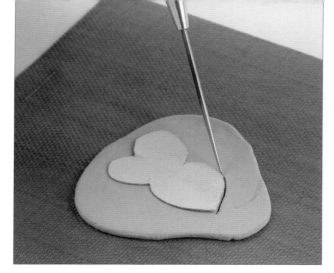

2 Roll out 10g (¹⁄₃oz) of silver clay to the thickness of five playing cards. Place the template of the mouse's head onto the clay and cut around it with a clay pick or craft knife.

3 Press the end of the needle file into the centre of each of the ears, to create an indent and to make the ears three-dimensional.

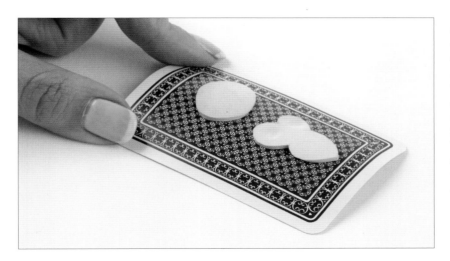

4 Roll out the remaining clay to a thickness of five playing cards. Place the template for the mouse's body onto the clay. Cut around the template with a clay pick or craft knife. Apply a thin layer of balm to the surface of a playing card. Place the two clay shapes onto the playing card. Bend the card slightly, so that it is curved. Allow the clay pieces to dry on the curved playing card for 45 minutes, so that they retain their shape.

5 After 45 minutes, remove the clay pieces from the playing card and allow them to dry thoroughly (see pages 24–25 for guidance). When the pieces are dry, sand and smooth the edges, backs and fronts with a sponge sanding pad. Use some polishing papers to give the pieces a really smooth finish.

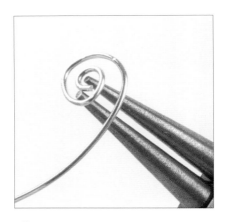

6 Take a length of fine silver wire measuring 2.5cm (1in). Use some round-nose pliers to create a loose coil for the mouse's tail. Leave a straight piece of wire at the end so that this can be embedded into the mouse's body.

7 Take a small piece of silver lump clay. Use a clay modelling tool to mix the clay with a little bit of water to create a thick paste.

8 Apply some paste to the back of the mouse's body, in the centre and out towards one edge. Place the end of the fine silver wire coil into the paste. Apply some paste on top of the wire. Use the clay modelling tool to cover the end of the wire completely. Smooth the back of the mouse with your finger or a wet paintbrush. Allow the piece to dry thoroughly.

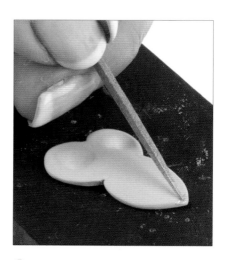

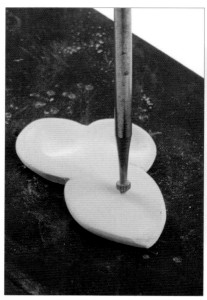

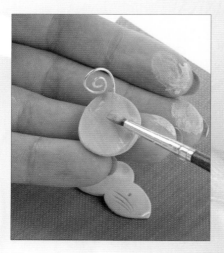

9 To make the nose of the mouse more defined, use a needle file to carve into the end of the nose. Do this gently because the clay has not yet been fired, so is still fragile.

10 Use a pin vice with a diamond burr to drill an indent into the dry clay to create the mouse's eye.

11 Use the end of a needle file to carve three lines across the face from the nose towards the ears. This gives the appearance of the mouse's whiskers. When the paste on the back of the mouse's body has dried, apply another layer of paste to cover up any of the silver wire that might be showing. Smooth the paste with a wet paintbrush. Allow the piece to dry out completely once again.

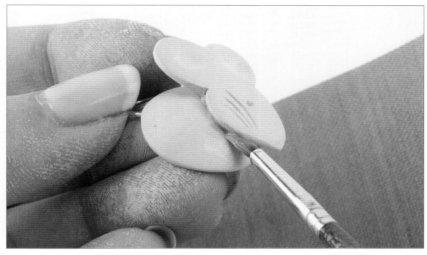

12 Apply a generous amount of silver syringe clay to the base of the back of the mouse's head.

13 Stick the head to the body, on the opposite side to the tail, pressing the clay down gently so that the two pieces are as closely aligned as possible. Use a wet paintbrush to remove any excess syringe clay around the edges of the piece. Allow the mouse to dry completely.

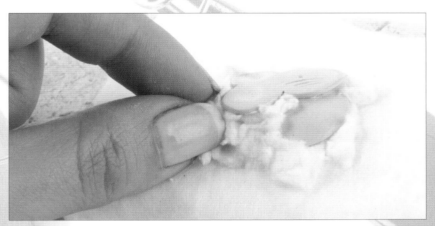

14 Use a sponge sanding pad and polishing papers to make sure the piece has a completely smooth finish before firing. Support the piece with some fibre blanket to preserve the curved shape and to prevent the clay from slumping during firing. Fire the mouse according to the instructions on pages 168–169.

15 After firing, allow the piece to cool or quench it in cold water. Brush the surface with a brass wire brush to reveal the silver. If you would like the piece to be shiny, use wet polishing papers and silver polish to bring the silver to a mirror-like shine.

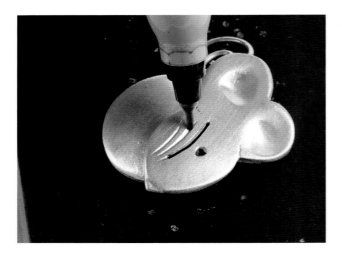

16 After you have finished brushing and polishing the piece, use a black, fine-line marker pen to blacken the whiskers and the indent of the eye.

17 Use the black marker pen to colour in the indent of the ears. Allow the ink to dry. To protect the ink from fading or wearing off you can coat the piece with metal varnish or rub some Renaissance wax over the surface.

18 Open a jump ring with some chain-nose pliers and attach it to the last loop in the acrylic chain. Attach a necklace clasp to the jump ring and close it with the pliers. Repeat this process at the other end of the acrylic chain.

19 Open a jump ring and attach this to the outer coil of the mouse's tail. Attach the jump ring to the middle of the acrylic chain. Close the jump ring securely and your necklace is complete. You may wish to make some more mice charms in silver, copper or bronze.

completing the set

Follow the same steps to make a mouse charm in copper and bronze. Instead of fine silver wire, use copper or bronze wire for the tails. Copper and bronze clays fire at a higher temperature, so fine silver wire might melt if you attached it to a copper or bronze piece before firing. See pages 168–169 for instructions on how to fire the copper and bronze mouse charms.

Scotty dog ring

I chose a Scotty dog as my second precious pet dog project. Scotties have such a strong and instantly recognisable silhouette, so this breed of dog was perfect for what I wanted to achieve with this simple ring shape. I have chosen to add a studded leather collar to my Scotty dog, but you can have fun adorning your own Scotty dog design any way you wish.

MATERIALS

Template (page 174), card and scissors
Clay balm
Teflon sheet
Playing cards
20g (¾oz) copper clay
Mini roller
Needle tool or craft knife
Circle cutter: you will need to work out what size ring you want, then add on two sizes
Sponge sanding pads
Polishing papers
Firing equipment
Pickling equipment
Wire brass brush
Agate burnisher
Small paintbrush
Piece of red leather, 2.5 x 0.5cm (1 x ¼in)
Leather glue
Silver-coloured embellishments

1 Draw a template for the ring (see page 174) onto a piece of card and cut this shape out.

2 Roll out 20g (¾oz) of copper clay to a thickness of seven playing cards. Place the Scotty dog template onto the clay and cut around it using a needle tool or craft knife.

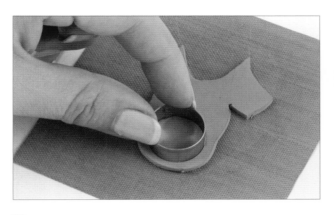

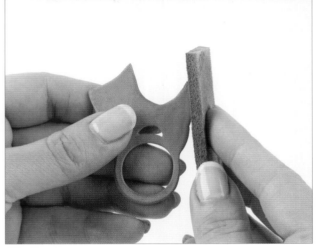

3 Cut out a hole from the centre of the bottom of the clay shape, two sizes bigger than the ring size you require. Use a clay pick or craft knife to cut a semi-circle out of the clay just above this ring hole. This gives the appearance of the dog having legs and standing on top of the ring.

4 Allow the piece to dry completely (see pages 24–25). Sand and smooth the ring using a sponge sanding pad and polishing papers.

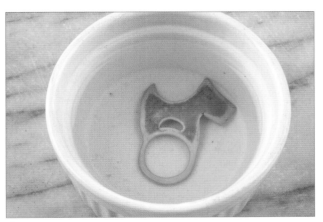

5 Fire the ring according to the instructions on pages 168–169. Allow the dog to cool or quench in cold water.

6 Place the ring in a pickle solution for between five and fifteen minutes to remove any firescale.

7 Use a wire brass brush to reveal the copper. Rinse the ring in warm water. Polish with an agate burnisher.

8 Cut a small piece of leather measuring 2.5 x 0.5cm (1 x ¼in) for the dog's collar.

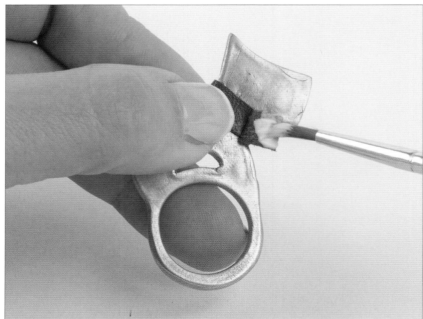

9 Apply some leather glue to the back of the piece of leather with a small paintbrush. Stick the leather around the neck of the dog and overlap the ends on the back of the piece.

10 Finish the ring by sticking some silver-coloured embellishments to the collar. Your ring is now ready to wear.

Rabbit pendant

No one can resist the cuteness of a bunny rabbit, so why not have a go at making your own precious metal version. This silver design is created by sculpting and carving the clay and adding sparkly precious gems. I have added a bow tie to my bunny and bent one of his ears over slightly to make him a little quirky and give him more personality.

MATERIALS

- Teflon sheet
- 10g (1/3oz) silver clay
- Curved needle file
- Small paintbrush
- Clay shaper tool
- Pencil
- Needle tool or craft knife
- Pin vice with diamond burr
- Silver syringe clay
- Cocktail stick
- Two clear cubic zirconia, 3mm (1/8in)
- One clear cubic zirconia, 2mm (1/16in)
- Clay balm
- Snake roller
- Cup of water
- Tissue blade
- Sponge sanding pads
- Polishing papers
- Firing equipment
- Wire brass brush
- Agate burnisher
- Sterling silver chain with clasp

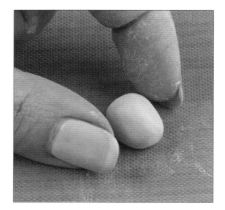

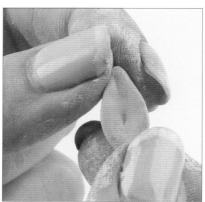

1 Roll a 4g (1/6oz) piece of silver clay into a ball to create the rabbit's head. Pinch the ball so that it is slightly oval-shaped and pointed at the front to form the nose. Set the piece aside to dry.

2 Take two small pieces of silver clay each weighing approximately 1g (3/100oz). Form the pieces of clay into diamond-like ear shapes. Pinch the ears at the top to make a pointed tip.

3 Press the clay ears around a curved needle file to make the inner ear concave and to add texture to the inner ears.

4 Gently bend one of the ears over at the top to form a right angle. Allow the ears to dry completely.

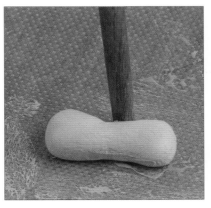

5 Make the bow tie by taking about 2g (⁷/₁₀₀oz) of the excess clay and forming it into a bow shape. Use some water to help you mould the clay more easily.

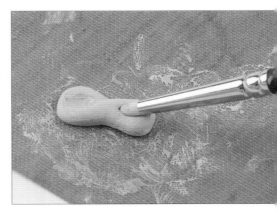

6 Use a clay shaper tool to indent the fold of the bow tie on each side. Allow the bow tie to dry out thoroughly.

7 Use a needle file to smooth the indents on the bow tie.

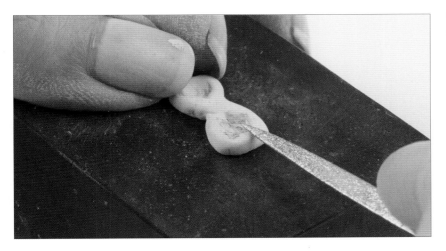

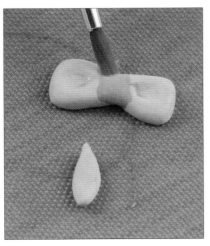

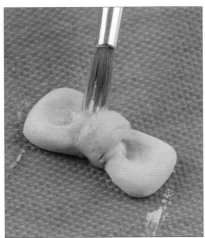

8 Take a small piece of clay and press it into a long, flat rectangle shape, with slightly tapered ends. Add some water to the middle of the bow tie with a paintbrush. Wrap the rectangle of clay around the bow tie to create the central knot.

9 Use a wet paintbrush to smooth the edges of the centre knot shape to the bow tie and seal them together.

10 When the ears have dried, sand the base of each so that it is flat. Use a needle file to sand the edges of each ear to create a bevelled edge.

11 When the head has completely dried, draw the shape of the nose and mouth onto the clay.

12 Use the pointed end of a needle file to carve the shape of the nose and mouth. Lightly smooth any rough areas or imperfections in the clay with a sponge sanding pad and polishing papers.

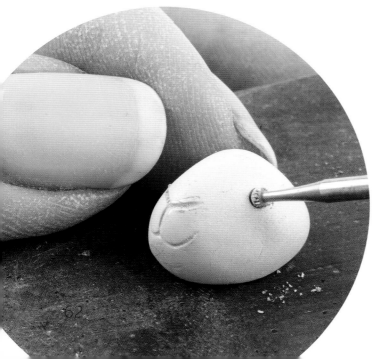

13 Drill the holes for the rabbit's eyes using a pin vice with a diamond burr. Drill holes that are wide enough for a 3mm (1/8in) cubic zirconia to sit inside. Drill the hole deep enough for the cubic zirconia to sit inside, so that the table of the stone (see page 91) is level with the top of the clay.

14 Apply a generous amount of syringe clay to the base of the straight ear.

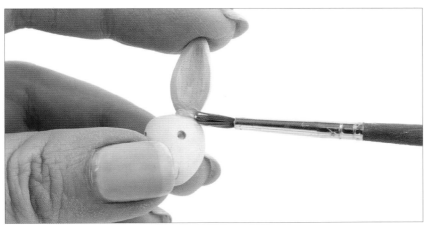

15 Attach the ear to the right-hand side of the head. Use a wet paintbrush to smooth the excess syringe clay and to ensure there is a strong seal between the ear and the head. Hold the ear in place for one minute to allow the syringe clay to dry and for the two pieces of clay to connect. Set the piece aside to dry for thirty minutes then repeat this process with the second ear.

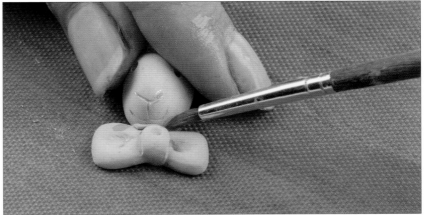

16 In the centre of the bow tie, drill a hole with the pin vice and diamond burr, deep enough for a 2mm (¹/₁₆in) cubic zirconia to sit inside the hole, so that the table of the stone is level with the top of the clay.

17 Apply a generous amount of syringe clay to the top of the bow tie. Stick the bow tie to the bottom of the rabbit's head. Use a damp paintbrush to smooth away any excess syringe clay and to seal the join between the two pieces. Allow the entire piece to dry fully.

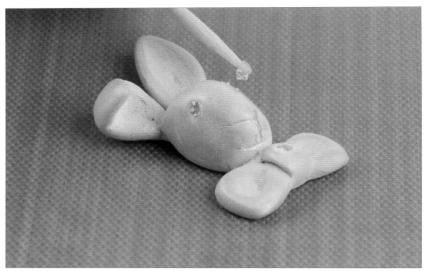

18 Add a little syringe clay into each of the eye holes and into the hole in the centre of the bow tie.

19 Dab the end of a cocktail stick with a little clay balm and use this to pick up the table top of the 3mm (¹⁄₈in) cubic zirconia. Insert the cubic zirconia into one of the eye holes. Push the cubic zirconia firmly down into the hole. Wipe away any excess clay with a damp baby wipe or small paintbrush. Repeat this process with the second eye and add the 2mm (¹⁄₁₆in) cubic zirconia to the hole in the bow tie.

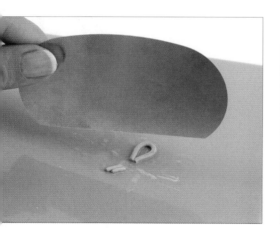

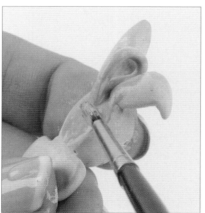

20 Roll a small piece of clay into a rope and form it into a loop. Trim off the ends to neaten. Allow the loop to dry.

21 When the loop is dry, stick this between the ears with some syringe clay to create a bail. Allow the piece to dry completely. Sand and smooth the whole piece before firing. Fire the rabbit pendant according to the instructions on pages 168–169.

22 After firing, allow the piece to cool. Do not quench it in cold water because this may damage the cubic zirconia. When the piece has cooled, brush it with a brass brush to reveal the silver. Use an agate burnisher to polish the edge of the ears, the face and the bow tie. Thread a silver necklace through the bail and your pendant is now ready to wear.

In the Jungle

Copper clay is such a richly coloured metal and lends itself beautifully to the jungle creatures in this section. Lions and elephants are always very popular animals for jewellery pieces and present the perfect opportunity to combine the warmth of copper with the coolness of silver. Here you will discover how to connect these metals in different ways. Copper clay works perfectly in capturing the smooth lines and coils of the snake ring and pendant, giving them a colourful and very modern look.

Techniques covered:

Snake pendant

Since the dawn of jewellery making, snakes have been used as inspiration for totems and talismans. Snakes were favoured as symbols by many cultures including the Celts, Native Americans, Maya, Aztecs, Romans and Ancient Egyptians. The snake is said to symbolise assertive power, fertility, healing, transformation, knowledge and intellect. Snakes are still very popular in modern jewellery. On a recent trip to Venice, I was inspired by the Murano glass snakes and decided to make my own in copper clay. Metal clay lends itself beautifully to creating fluid shapes and this is where the ability to sculpt the copper has huge advantages over traditional metalsmithing.

MATERIALS

Ceramic tile

Snake roller

14g (½oz) copper clay

Cup of water

Paintbrush

Sponge sanding pad

Polishing papers

Pencil

Pin vice with diamond burr drill bit

Firing equipment

Pickling equipment

Metal tongs

Pearlescent paint, ruby red

Bead of your choice, 8mm (5/16in)

Copper-coloured head pin, 5cm (2in)

Suede cord in the colour of your choice

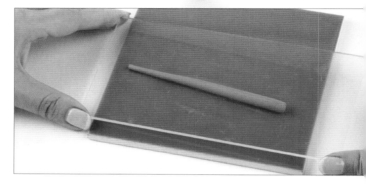

1 Use a snake roller to roll out the copper clay on top of the ceramic tile. While you are rolling, apply more pressure to the bottom end of the shape to create a snake-like shape. This allows the clay to remain thicker at the top of the snake, where its head will be. Roll the snake to a length of approximately 10cm (4in).

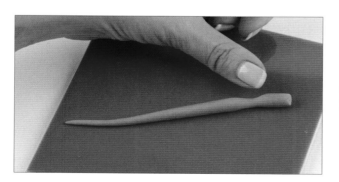

2 With your fingers, roll the end of the snake to a point to form the tail. Make an indent with your finger at the top of the snake to form the neck and the head.

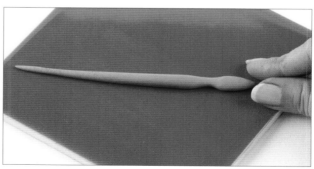

3 Pinch the head of the snake to create its pointed face. Mould the clay until you are happy with the shape and definition of the head and neck.

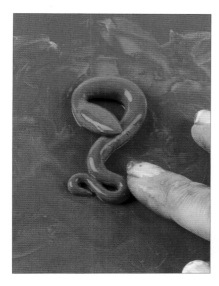

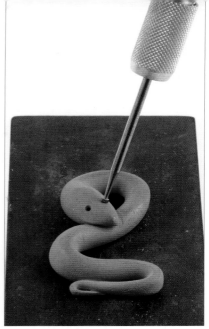

4 Use a wet paintbrush to soak the entire snake with water. Leave the snake for three minutes and allow the water to saturate the clay. This makes the snake much more malleable. Use your fingers or a wet paintbrush to move the clay into the coiled snake shape. Place the face on top of one of the coils of the body to form a secure loop. Form a loop at the base of the tail with the clay.

5 Allow the clay to dry completely. This may take longer than usual, depending on how much water you added in step 4. After the piece has dried, sand and finish it with a sponge pad and dry polishing papers to make the snake as smooth as possible.

6 Mark where you would like the eyes of the snake with a pencil. Use a pin vice with a diamond burr drill bit to drill each of the eye holes.

7 Place the snake inside a steel firing box on top of a 3cm (1¼in) layer of coconut-activated carbon. Fire the snake at 350ºC (662ºF) for ten minutes.

8 After the first stage of firing, remove the steel box from the kiln. The piece will now have a blackened appearance, as shown.

9 Cover the piece completely with a layer of coconut-activated carbon. Place the lid on the steel box, then fire the snake for thirty minutes at 900°C (1652°F). After the piece has been fired, open the kiln door slightly and allow the box to cool down inside the kiln. This can take up to three or four hours.

10 When the box has cooled, remove it from the kiln and place it on a heat-resistant surface. Open the lid of the box and move some of the granules of carbon around with some metal tongs; if they are still glowing, allow them to cool completely.

11 After the carbon granules have cooled, remove the piece from the box with a pair of metal tongs. Quench the piece in cold water before handling. Place the snake in a pickle solution for between five and fifteen minutes to remove any firescale. Brush the snake with a brass wire brush to reveal the copper.

12 Add a drop of pearlescent paint to each of the eyes. Allow the paint to dry. Thread a bead onto a head pin and attach it to the loop at the end of the tail by making a wrapped loop with the excess wire. Knot a piece of suede cord through the top loop in the neck and your snake pendant is ready to wear.

Snake ring

The snake's coiling shape makes it ideal for a ring. Here is a simple project using the same techniques as the snake pendant, but this time it is a piece to adorn your finger. I have wrapped the snake-shaped clay around a mandrel to form a simple ring shape. If you prefer you can make the snake longer and form it into coils that extend along the finger: the choice is yours.

MATERIALS

Ring-sizing tool
Wooden ring mandrel
Ring-sizing paper
Ceramic tile
Snake roller
7g (¼oz) copper clay
Cup of water
Small paintbrush
Pencil
Pin vice with diamond burr drill bit
Sponge sanding pad
Polishing papers
Firing equipment
Pickling equipment
Metal tongs
Pearlescent paint, ruby red

1 Measure the finger that you want to create the ring for. The copper clay shrinks by approximately six per cent during firing so your copper ring needs to be created two sizes bigger than you actually need. Place a ring-sizing paper around the wooden mandrel at the place on the mandrel that corresponds with the correct ring size.

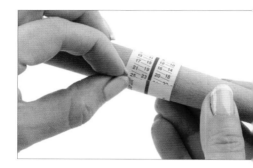

2 Use a snake roller to roll the copper clay into a snake shape on top of a ceramic tile. While you are rolling, apply more pressure to the bottom end of the snake. This allows the clay to remain thicker at the top of the snake, where its head will be. Roll the snake to a length of approximately 5cm (2in).

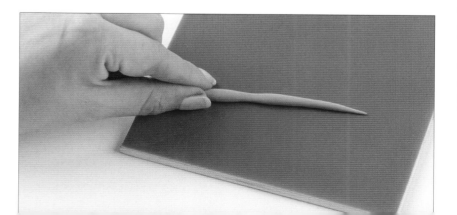

3 With your fingers, roll the end of the snake to a point to form the tail. Make an indent with your finger at the top of the snake to form the neck and the head. Pinch the head of the snake to create its pointed face. Wet the clay using a paintbrush.

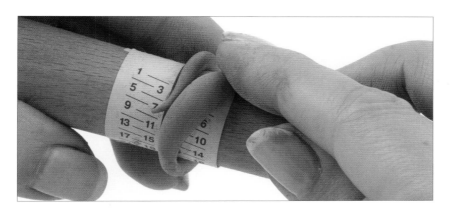

4 Take the clay snake and wrap it around the ring mandrel on top of the ring-sizing paper. Make sure that the clay is positioned along the solid black line in the centre of the paper. Position the clay so that the head of the snake is pointing downwards and so that the tail is resting on top of the head and curling upwards.

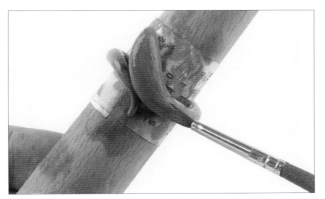

5 Use a wet paintbrush to smooth the surface of the clay. Allow the snake to dry in place on the mandrel for an hour. After an hour, gently remove the snake from the mandrel and allow it to dry out completely. You will need to allow a longer drying time because you have added extra water to the clay.

6 After the piece has dried, place it back onto the mandrel to hold it steady. Use a pencil to mark where you would like the eyes to be. Use a pin vice with a diamond burr to drill the holes for the eyes.

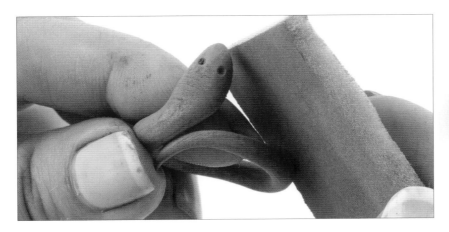

7 Sand and finish the snake ring with a sponge pad and dry polishing papers to make the clay as smooth as possible and to remove any imperfections. Fire the ring according to the instructions on pages 168–169.

8 After firing, allow the ring to cool. Place the ring in a pickle solution for between five and fifteen minutes to remove any firescale. After pickling, brush with a brass wire brush to reveal the copper. Add some pearlescent paint to the eyes to complete the ring.

Elephant pendant

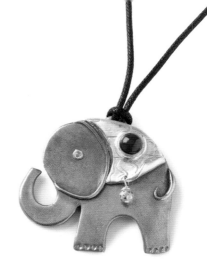

Elephants are such majestic creatures and they make wonderful pieces of jewellery. I wanted this piece to have a tribal look and feel to it; the copper clay works wonderfully for this. Adding a silver blanket gives this elephant a touch of additional glamour and the fine silver cup bezel allows you to set any stone or glass cabochon quickly and easily after firing. Elephants are said to symbolise protection, good luck and wisdom, so what better reason could you need to create your own precious metal elephant?

MATERIALS

Template (page 174), card and scissors

Teflon sheet

Clay balm

50g (1¾oz) copper clay

Mini roller

Playing cards

Clay pick or craft knife

Sponge sanding pad

Needle file

Ceramic tile

Snake roller

Small paintbrush

Cup of water

Pencil

Pin vice with diamond burr drill bit

Polishing papers

Firing equipment

Pickling equipment

Brass wire brush

7g (¼oz) silver clay

Tribal-style texture sheet

Silver syringe clay

Baby wipe

Fine silver cup bezel (to fit the cabochon of your choice)

One clear cubic zirconia, 2mm (1/16in)

Drinking straw

Flat-back cabochon (the size of your choice)

Jewellery glue

Bezel setting tool

Metal burnisher

Gold-coloured aluminium bead, 4mm (3/16in)

Gold-coloured head pin, 5cm (2in)

Round-nose pliers

Wire cutters

Black leather cord (the length of your choice)

1 Draw the elephant shape (see page 174) onto a piece of card and cut it out. This will be your template. Apply a thin layer of clay balm to a teflon sheet. Roll out the copper clay to a thickness of seven playing cards. Place the elephant template on top of the clay. Cut around the template shape with a clay pick or craft knife.

2 Set the elephant aside to dry thoroughly according to the instructions on pages 24–25. After the piece has dried, sand and smooth the edges, front and back of the elephant with a sponge sanding pad. Use a needle file to refine the clay in the gap between the trunk and the head to remove any imperfections.

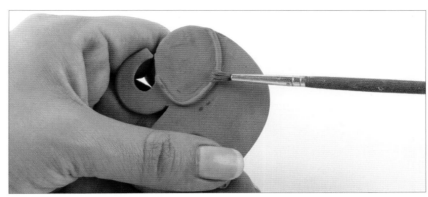

3 Take a small piece of the excess copper clay and roll it into a thin rope of clay measuring approximately 5cm (2in) long.

4 Wet the rope of clay with a small paintbrush. Carefully pick up the rope of clay with a wet paintbrush and place it onto the elephant's head. Guide the rope of clay with the paintbrush so that it curves from the top of the head to the base of the trunk to form the elephant's ear. Smooth the clay with the wet paintbrush to seal the two pieces of clay together.

5 Allow the clay to dry once more, then sand and smooth the face and body of the elephant with a sanding sponge and polishing papers. Use a needle file to carve the toe nails of the elephant on each foot.

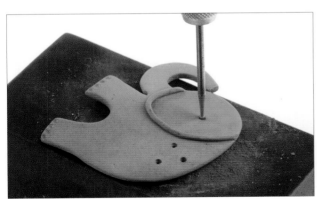

6 Mark the elephant's eye with a pencil, then drill a hole through the clay. You need to drill right through to the other side. Drill three holes through the clay at the top of the body. These holes will be used after the copper clay has been fired to plug the silver clay blanket into.

7 Take a small piece of copper clay and roll it into a short, tapered sausage shape. Wet it and stick it on the right-hand side of the elephant's body to create a tail. Use a wet paintbrush to seal the two pieces together and to curve the clay shape, so that the tail appears to sweep upwards.

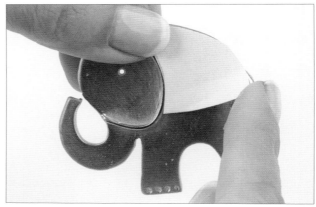

8 Allow the clay to dry completely. Fire the elephant according to the instructions on pages 168–169. After firing, allow the elephant to cool, then place it in a pickle solution to remove any firescale. Brush the elephant with a wire brush to reveal the copper.

9 Draw the blanket shape (see page 174) onto a piece of card and cut this out. Check that the card shape fits your fired elephant perfectly and trim the card if necessary.

10 Apply a thin layer of balm to a teflon sheet. Roll out 7g (¼oz) of silver clay to a thickness of five playing cards. Apply some clay balm to a texture sheet and press this onto the rolled out clay.

11 Place the blanket template onto the silver clay and cut around it with a clay pick or craft knife. Place the silver clay onto the fired copper elephant and press down gently all over the blanket.

12 Lift the right-hand edge of the silver clay blanket and curl it upwards. Hold this in place for one minute to allow the clay to maintain this position. This will give the blanket a more three-dimensional appearance when it has been fired. It also ensures that there is a gap between the bottom edge of the blanket and the elephant so that you can attach the bead after firing.

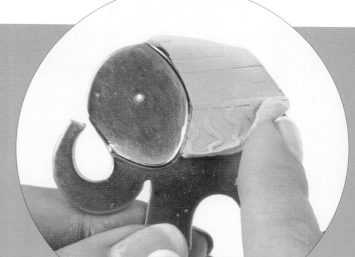

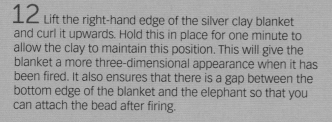

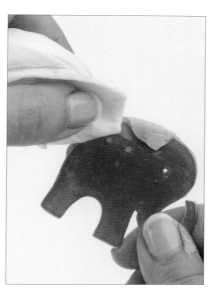

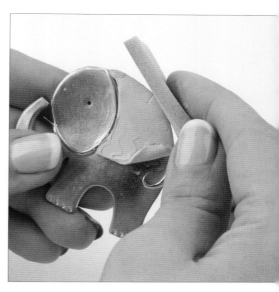

13 To ensure that the silver clay adheres well to the copper after firing, wrap the top of the blanket over the copper elephant. Apply some silver syringe clay to the holes on the back of the elephant.

14 Ensure that the syringe clay has a good connection with the silver clay blanket on the other side of the elephant. Wipe away any excess silver syringe clay from with a damp baby wipe.

15 Allow the clay to dry completely. Gently sand and smooth the blanket with a sponge sanding pad.

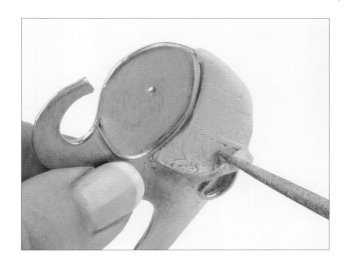

16 Use a needle file to refine the edges of the blanket, including the right-hand edge that is curled upwards. The needle file enables you to access the smaller spaces between the clay.

17 Very gently and carefully, use a pin vice to drill a hole in the middle of the blanket at the bottom edge of the blanket. This is where you will attach the bead after firing.

Key Technique: creating a bezel before firing

The simplest way to create a bezel before firing your piece is to attach a cup bezel. This is a bezel that is made from fine silver and is a complete made-to-measure 'cup' shape. Simply attach the cup to fired or unfired silver with silver paste or syringe clay. After drying, fire the piece. The two pieces of silver will fuse together. The bezel cup retains its shape and size after firing so there is no need to do any calculations or allow for additional shrinkage. Select a cabochon that fits into the bezel cup before firing. After firing, place the cabochon inside the bezel cup and use a bezel setting tool and metal burnisher to set the cabochon securely within the bezel.

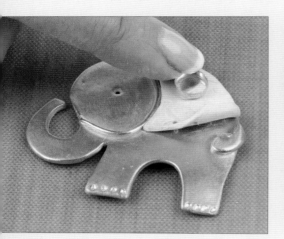 

18 Apply a generous amount of silver syringe clay to the base of the bezel cup and place this on top of the silver clay blanket. Press down gently to adhere the bezel to the dried clay. Use a wet paintbrush to remove any excess clay around the base of the cup and to ensure there is a good seal.

19 Roll a thin rope of silver clay and place this around the base of the bezel cup. Smooth the join between the ends of the rope of clay with a wet paintbrush.

Key Technique: inserting a small stone before firing

Certain gemstones can be inserted into metal clays before firing. Check the charts on pages 170–172 to see which natural gemstones and cubic zirconia can withstand the heat of firing.

20 Apply some silver syringe clay to the eyehole of the elephant.

21 Dip the end of a cocktail stick into some clay balm. Use this to pick up the flat top of the cubic zirconia. Place the cubic zirconia into the silver clay within the elephant's eye hole. Press the cubic zirconia down fully into the clay so that the top of it is level with the top of the clay.

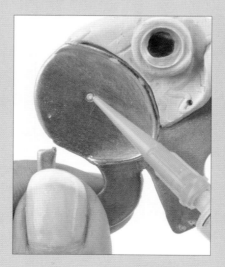 

22 Allow the clay to dry fully, then sand and smooth the silver clay areas of the elephant. Wipe away any unwanted silver clay smudges from the copper with a baby wipe.

23 Re-fire the elephant according to the instructions on pages 168–169. After firing, brush the silver parts of the elephant with a wire brass brush.

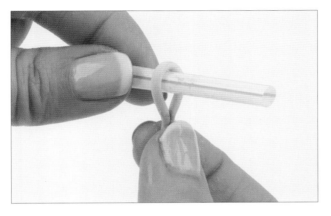

24 Roll some excess silver clay into a rope and bend this over a drinking straw to form a loop for the elephant's bail. Pinch the ends of the clay together and seal them in place with some water or a little silver syringe clay.

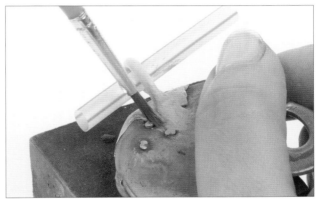

25 Allow the silver clay bail to dry. After drying, attach the bail to the back of the elephant with a generous amount of silver syringe clay. Use a paintbrush to seal the silver clay bail to the fired silver on the back of the piece.

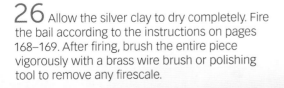

26 Allow the silver clay to dry completely. Fire the bail according to the instructions on pages 168–169. After firing, brush the entire piece vigorously with a brass wire brush or polishing tool to remove any firescale.

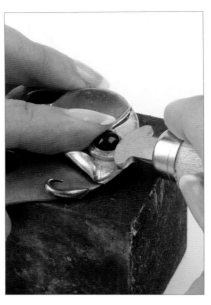

27 Add a drop of jewellery glue to the bottom of the bezel cup. Place your chosen cabochon inside the bezel cup. Allow the glue to set.

28 Use a bezel setting tool to push the edges of the bezel tightly around the cabochon. Work from opposite edges of the bezel.

29 Use a curved metal burnisher to smooth the edges of the bezel cup and ensure that they grip the cabochon securely.

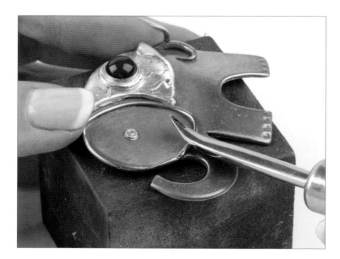

30 Use the metal burnisher to bring a high shine to the edges of the elephant, the raised tail and the ear shape.

31 Thread a gold-coloured bead onto a head pin. Bend the wire to a right angle at the top of the bead, then bend the wire back over a pair of round-nose pliers to create a loop. Thread the head pin through the hole at the base of the silver blanket. Wrap the excess head pin wire around the base of the loop and trim any excess wire. Knot a piece of leather cord through the bail and your elephant pendant is now ready to wear.

Alternative metal-mixing examples:
overlaying silver onto copper or bronze

Although silver, copper and bronze all fire at different temperatures, these different metals can all be combined in one piece of jewellery. Each metal must be fired in different stages. It is essential that the copper or bronze is fired first because both of these fire at a hotter temperature than silver clay. Add the silver clay to the fired piece of copper or bronze and then fire the entire piece at a temperature that is safe for the silver. Re-firing the copper or bronze clay will not affect it, although you may have to polish away any additional firescale.

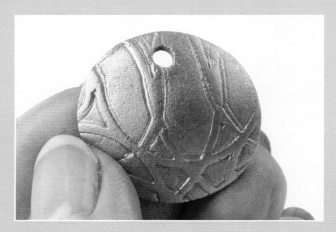

1 Create the copper or bronze clay design you would like, then fire, pickle and brush the piece.

2 Roll out the silver clay and attach it to the piece of fired copper or bronze clay, in the desired design.

3 Ensure that you wrap the silver clay around the fired copper or bronze piece so that it encapsulates it.

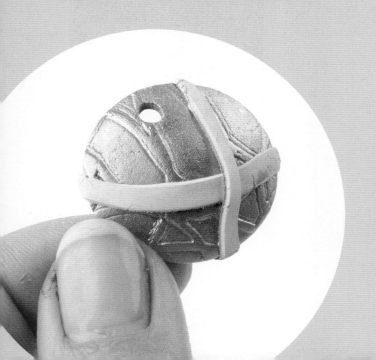

4 When the silver clay has dried, fire it with a gas torch, on a gas hob or in a kiln in the usual way. When the silver fires it shrinks and will attach itself securely to the copper or bronze piece beneath.

Alternative metal-mixing examples: using silver plugs

If you prefer to add just an accent of silver clay to a piece of fired copper or bronze clay, this is the ideal method to use. Make holes in the piece of copper or bronze before firing. After firing and finishing the piece you can feed the silver clay into the holes. The silver clay will attach itself to the copper or bronze. After firing the silver clay in the normal way, you will be left with a lovely silver accent.

1 Make your chosen design from copper or bronze clay. Drill holes into the dried clay. Fire the copper or bronze piece in the normal way, then pickle and brush it.

2 Create a slim sausage of silver clay and feed this through the holes of the fired metal. Ensure that the silver completely fills the hole without any gaps. Use your fingers to push the silver clay firmly into place.

3 Use some silver syringe clay to seal the holes at the back. Allow the silver clay to dry. Sand and smooth the dried clay. Fire the piece again using the appropriate method and timings for silver clay.

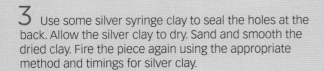

4 After firing, brush and polish the entire piece again. You may need to polish the bronze or copper clay to remove any firescale.

Lion bracelet

When I first came up with the idea of a book about metal clay animals, a lion was immediately on my shortlist. Not only are lions incredibly beautiful but symbolically they are power animals, representing strength, courage and confidence. Making a lion also gave me the opportunity to combine bronze and silver, and what a perfect combination they make here. The face is created by sculpting the bronze clay. If you have never done this before then don't panic. The facial features are added in layers. If the lion is not looking how you want, simply refine or remove the clay. Add the layers and keep making modifications until you are happy with the results.

MATERIALS

50g (1¾oz) bronze clay
Teflon sheet
Cup of water
Clay shaper tool
Sponge sanding pad
Needle file
Rubber block
Pin vice
Firing equipment
Pickling equipment
Brass wire brush
Clay balm
20g (¾oz) silver clay
Clay pick or craft knife
Ceramic tile
Snake roller
Small paintbrush
Leather cuff
Awl
Small gold- and silver-
   coloured beads
20cm (8in) silver wire,
   0.6mm gauge

1 Take a 50g (1¾oz) piece of bronze clay and place it on top of a teflon sheet. Pinch off 10g (⅓oz) of the clay and set it aside. Smooth and mould the large piece of clay into a rounded patty shape with your fingers. Make sure that the clay remains thick.

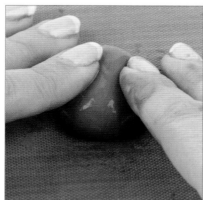

2 Press the clay down with your fingers to create the eye sockets and to form the bridge of the lion's nose. Wet your fingers and smooth the water over the clay to make it more malleable and easier to sculpt.

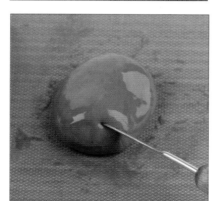

3 When you have achieved the desired shape of the nose and face, use a clay modelling tool to poke a hole in the clay for each of the lion's nostrils.

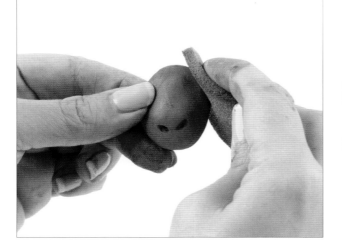
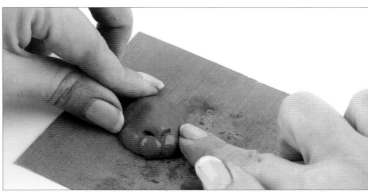

4 Allow the clay to dry out for a couple of hours in a warm place, or allow it to dry out overnight if drying at room temperature. Sand the clay with a sponge sanding pad to create a smooth surface and to modify the face shape if necessary.

5 Place the piece on a teflon sheet and wet the surface of the clay. Take the 10g (1/3oz) piece of bronze clay and pinch off two small pieces. Roll them into balls and place them under the lion's nose. Smooth the clay with water to form the shape of the muzzle beneath the nose.

6 Allow to dry out completely. Use a needle file to open the holes up for the nostrils.

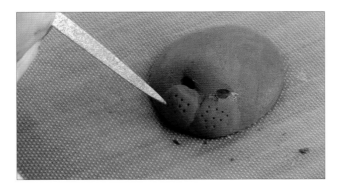

7 Use the pointed end of the needle file to create the holes where the lion's whiskers would be. Mark out the line of the mouth with the needle file.

8 Take the excess bronze clay and flatten it into an oval shape. Wet the back of the lion's head and clay oval and press the two pieces together. Add more water to seal the join between the two pieces of clay. Push this additional clay around the edges of the face to create a frame, enabling you to add the mane when the piece has been fired (see steps 9 and 10 for reference).

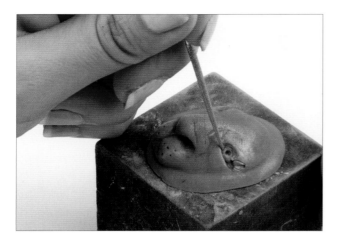

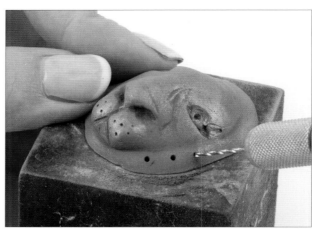

9 Allow the piece to dry completely. After drying, place on top of a rubber block. Use the end of a needle file to carve the eyes out of the dry clay.

10 Take a pin vice and drill holes through the clay at intervals around the edge of the face. These are the holes that you will plug the silver clay into when the bronze face has been fired.

11 Sand and smooth the lion's face with a sponge sanding pad and dry polishing papers. As you can see, it doesn't matter if any small areas around the holes break off. Fire the bronze clay according to the instructions on pages 168–169.

12 After firing, allow the lion's face to cool completely. Place the piece in a pickle solution to remove any firescale.

13 Brush the fired piece of bronze clay with a brass wire brush to reveal the metal.

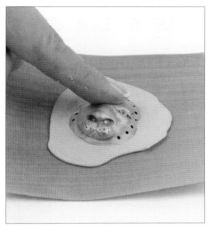

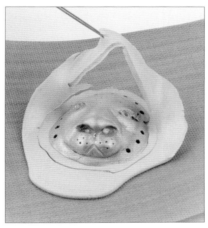

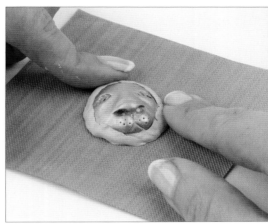

14 Add a layer of clay balm to a teflon sheet. Roll out 20g (¾oz) of silver clay to a thickness of five playing cards. Place the bronze lion's face in the centre of the rolled out clay and press down gently.

15 Cut around the outline of the lion's face with a clay pick or craft knife, leaving a margin of around 5mm (¼in). Remove the excess clay.

16 Push the excess clay up around the edge of the bronze lion. Press the silver clay so that it makes good contact with the fired bronze clay and fills the holes around the edge of the lion's face.

17 Take a small piece of the excess silver clay, place it on top of a ceramic tile and roll it into a rope of clay with a snake roller. Roll the rope to a length of approximately 5cm (2in). Roll the ends of the rope with your fingers to form points. Cut the rope of clay in two.

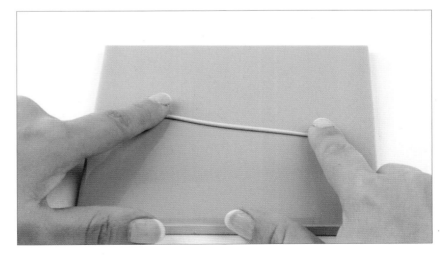

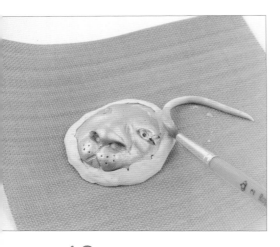

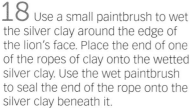

18 Use a small paintbrush to wet the silver clay around the edge of the lion's face. Place the end of one of the ropes of clay onto the wetted silver clay. Use the wet paintbrush to seal the end of the rope onto the silver clay beneath it.

19 Form the pointed end of the rope into a curl. Don't make all the curls too tight: ensure that you leave some gaps so that you can thread wire through after firing the piece. Repeat this process with the other half of the clay rope, placing it on the left-hand side of the head.

20 Continue rolling ropes from the excess silver clay. Position them around the lion's face, sealing them to the clay beneath with water. Vary the length and thickness of the ropes. Allow the piece to dry completely. Use a sponge sanding pad and needle file to refine the dry clay and remove any excess or imperfections.

21 Fire the silver clay according to the instructions on pages 168–169. After firing, brush the mane and back of the piece to reveal the silver. Brush the lion's face and use some metal polish to remove any firescale. Make two holes in a leather cuff using an awl; use the lion's face as a guide to judge how far apart to space them. Thread some silver wire through the holes in the lion's mane to attach it to the holes in the leather cuff. Attach some gold- and silver-coloured beads to the top of the lion's head with wire and secure the wire through the holes in the mane.

Alternative stone-setting techniques: using a claw setting

You can set stones inside a 'claw' type setting by embedding fine silver wire into silver clay before firing. After firing, the wire can be bent to hold the stone in place. This can also be done by using copper wire in copper clay and bronze wire in bronze clay.

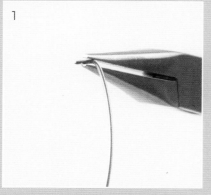

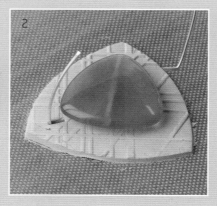

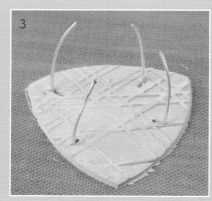

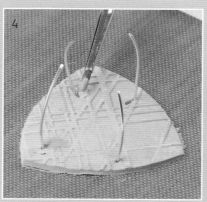

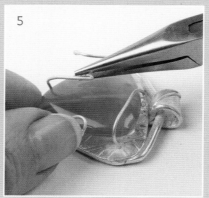

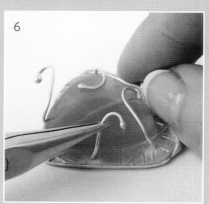

1 Take short lengths of wire and bend them so they are slightly curved. Fold the ends of the wire at 90-degree angles to form 'feet' – these will be embedded into the clay base and securely shrink-locked into place.

2 So that you can judge the spacing, place the cabochon you want to set onto the wet clay base and embed the feet of your wire claws into the clay around the edges of the stone. The wire claws won't shrink, but the clay in which they are embedded will, so leave a little space around the stone to allow for shrinkage.

3 After you have spaced the wire claws evenly around the edges of the cabochon stone, gently remove it.

4 Seal and strengthen the areas around each 'foot' with silver paste clay. Use a small paintbrush so that you can apply the paste accurately without spoiling any textures or patterns on your base piece.

5 Dry and fire the clay. Brush the piece to reveal the silver and do any polishing before setting the stone. Place the stone within the claws and gently bend them into place, taking care not to twist them.

6 Ensure that the claws are spaced in an even and pleasing manner, with the ends curled for an extra decorative flourish. Ensure that the stone is completely secure before you wear the piece.

Alternative stone-setting techniques: inserting a larger stone before firing

Due to the varying properties of gemstones, some can withstand the high firing temperatures of metal clay, while others cannot – refer to the charts on pages 170–172 to find out whether your chosen stone can be set before firing, or whether you should fire the metal first and insert the stone after.

Check the height of your stone before you begin. You'll need to add enough clay to the setting area – or embed the stone deeply enough in thicker clay pieces – to cover the stone's girdle by about 1–2mm (1/16in). During firing the metal clay will shrink and lock the stone into the metal.

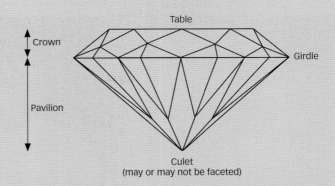

Table
Crown
Girdle
Pavilion
Culet
(may or may not be faceted)

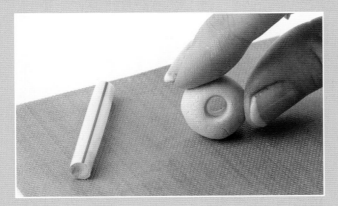

1 Create a ball of clay, then push a drinking straw through the centre to create a hole: cutting a hole in the clay under the stone helps minimise the amount that the clay pushes up as it shrinks.

2 Use a hard, flat surface such as a snake roller to embed the stone evenly into the clay ball.

3 Ensure that the girdle of the stone is embedded 1–2mm (1/16in) below the surface of the clay, and that the table of the stone is level.

4 Use a circular cutter to trim the edges of the bezel so that you have neat, vertical sides. Attach the bezel to your desired piece of jewellery before firing. After firing, cover the stone with a piece of masking tape before brushing and polishing, to avoid scratching it.

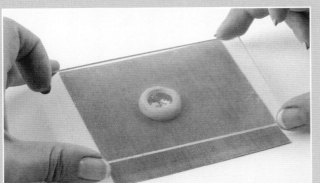

Feathered Friends

In this section you will discover how to immortalise beautiful birds in fine silver. Fashion your own nimble swallow into a ring, make an elegant swan brooch and capture the colourful majesty of these tropical birds. Who would have imagined just how inspiring our feathered friends could be?

Techniques covered:

- Ring-making using a ring core 94
- Using liver of sulphur 100
- Adding gold leaf 106
- Using coloured pencils and UV gel 113
- Other colour techniques 116

Swallow ring

Swallows are such graceful, agile birds. The only way to depict a swallow is in flight, soaring away to its next adventure. This ring is so fun to make and you could also use the same techniques to make a beautiful matching pendant.

MATERIALS

Fine silver ring core in the size of your choice
30g (1oz) silver clay
Teflon sheet
Mini roller
Clay balm
Playing cards
Texture sheet
Tissue blade
Cup of water
Clay shaper tool
Sponge sanding pad
Polishing papers
Template (page 174), scissors and card

Clay pick or craft knife
Silver syringe clay
Silver paste clay
Small paintbrush
Pin vice
Fibre blanket
Firing equipment
Wire ring brush
Liver of sulphur
Instant caffeinated coffee
Tweezers
Silver polish
Soft cloth

Key Technique: ring-making using a ring core

Metal clays shrink during firing, so when making rings with metal clay you need to make them slightly bigger to allow for this (see pages 130–131). Ring cores are a fantastic way of creating precious metal rings without all of the guesswork involved with creating a ring from scratch. Metal clays are also softer than sheet metal, so not only do ring cores give you the benefit of the perfect fit every time, they are much stronger and keep their perfectly round shape after firing.

1 Ring cores are available to buy in copper, bronze and fine silver and are available in a variety of widths and ring sizes. Choose the exact ring size that fits your finger; there is no need to allow for any shrinkage.

2 Measure the circumference of your ring core with a piece of paper or string. Roll out a length of clay that is long enough to completely encircle the ring core. The ring core itself is very strong, so the clay acts as surface decoration. You can roll the clay out as thinly as you like.

3 Add any texture or pattern that you would like to appear on the ring.

4 Trim the clay to the width of the ring core cavity with a tissue blade.

5 Carefully place the strip of silver clay around the ring core.

6 Seal the edges of the clay to the ring core with some water and a clay shaper tool. Allow the clay to dry fully.

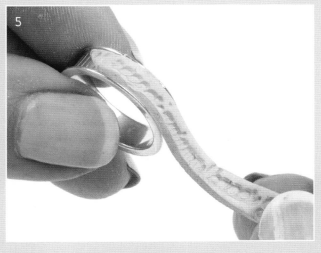

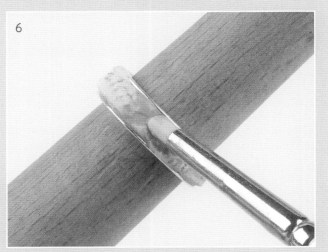

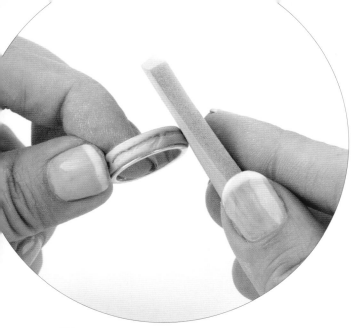

7 Sand and smooth the clay around the ring core with a sponge sanding pad and dry polishing papers. Do not worry about the area where the clay ends join, as you will be covering this up when you attach the swallow.

8 Take some of the excess silver clay and form it into the head and body of the swallow. Wet the clay to make it more malleable and easier to sculpt.

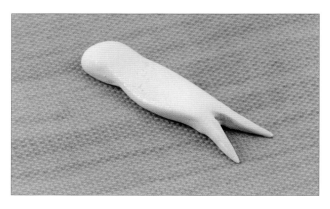

9 Stretch out the clay to elongate the swallow's body and tail. Press the clay down in the centre of the body to flatten it slightly. Make an incision in the clay with a tissue blade at the base of the body. Mould the clay to create the pointed ends of the swallow's tail. Set the clay aside to dry.

10 Draw the swallow's wing onto a piece of card and cut this out to create a template (see page 174).

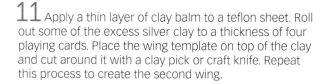

11 Apply a thin layer of clay balm to a teflon sheet. Roll out some of the excess silver clay to a thickness of four playing cards. Place the wing template on top of the clay and cut around it with a clay pick or craft knife. Repeat this process to create the second wing.

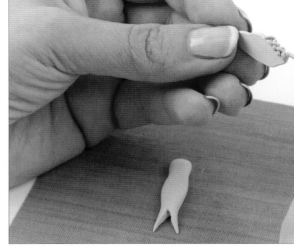

12 Allow the wings to dry completely. Sand and smooth the wings and the body after drying to remove any imperfections.

13 Apply a generous layer of syringe clay to the straight edge of the swallow's wing. Attach it to one side of the swallow's body – at the angle shown in the image below – and remove any excess clay with a wet paintbrush. Repeat this process to attach the second wing.

14 Rest the swallow to dry on a teflon sheet. Place some piles of playing cards on either side of the swallow to support its wings while they are drying. Allow the piece to dry completely.

15 To create the effect of feathers on the body and wings, apply a generous layer of paste clay all over the swallow with a paintbrush.

16 Use your finger or a cocktail stick to create a stippled effect on the body and wings.

17 After drying, gently smooth away any rough areas on the swallow with dry polishing papers. The stippled paste clay can feel quite rough and may be uncomfortable to wear when the ring has been fired. Run your finger over the entire piece to ensure there are no sharp areas sticking out.

18 Take a small piece of silver clay and mould it into a pointed beak shape that is flat at one end. Allow the beak to dry.

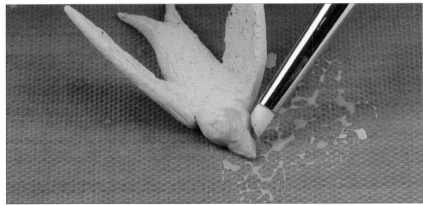

19 Attach the beak to the head of the swallow with some syringe clay. Use a clay shaper tool and a little water to seal the two pieces of clay together. Allow the swallow to dry completely.

20 Mark where you would like the eyes to be with a pencil. Use a pin vice to drill each eye hole.

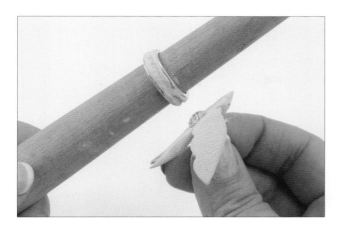

21 Apply a generous amount of syringe clay to the area on the ring where the clay ends are joined. Attach the swallow to the ring.

22 Use a wet paintbrush to smooth any excess syringe clay and to seal the two pieces together. Add more syringe clay if necessary. Allow the ring to dry completely.

23 Do any final sanding and smoothing of the swallow ring. Support the wings of the swallow with some fibre blanket to prevent them from slumping during firing. Fire the swallow according to the instructions on pages 168–169.

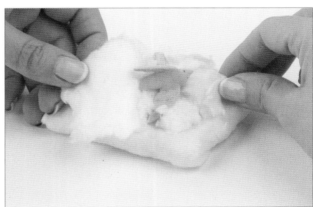

24 After firing, allow the ring to cool or quench it in cold water. Brush the ring and the swallow with a wire brush to reveal the silver.

Key Technique: using liver of sulphur

This technique will give a lovely aged look to your silver piece. If you'd prefer to keep your ring looking bright silver, simply polish it, and it's ready to wear.

25 Add a teaspoon of caffeinated instant coffee to a bowl of hot water and stir to dissolve.

26 Add a few drops of liquid liver of sulphur to the mixture. Stir well.

27 Hold the ring with a pair of tweezers and dip the swallow into the liver of sulphur solution. Keep lifting the swallow out of the solution to check on the colour. The caffeinated liver of sulphur solution creates an interesting patina on the silver.

28 When you are happy with the depth of colour, place the entire ring in a bowl of cold water. This neutralises the liver of sulphur and stops it from colouring any further.

29 Apply some silver polish all over the swallow and remove it with a soft cloth. This will take away the excess colour of the patina on the surface of the metal. The colour remains in the grooves and recesses of the silver, giving the swallow definition and creating an antique silver effect.

Swan brooch

The idea for this design came from a pair of emerald encrusted hoop earrings I saw an actress wearing in a magazine. The earrings were huge and I remember thinking how much I loved the shape of them and how they would make a lovely brooch. I tore out the magazine page and put it in my scrapbook. A couple of years later, this image became the inspiration for my swan design. Swans are such elegant creatures with their long, slender necks and beautiful body shape. The neck on this piece enables you to use it as a bail so that the piece could switch between being worn as a brooch or a pendant.

MATERIALS

Template (page 174), scissors and card
Clay balm
Teflon sheet
20g (¾oz) silver clay
Playing cards
Mini roller
Clay pick or craft knife
Round cutters, large and medium

Tissue blade
Sponge sanding pad
Silver syringe clay
Round needle file
Small paintbrush
Cup of water
Polishing papers
Fine silver brooch setting
Firing equipment
Brass wire brush
Gold leaf

Gas torch
Fire brick
Fine tweezers
Metal burnishing tool
Chain-nose pliers
Wire cutters
Metal file
½m (20in) silver wire, 0.6mm gauge
Strand of peridot green faceted glass crystal beads, 6mm (¼in)

1 Draw the swan head and neck shape onto a piece of card and cut this out (see page 174). Apply a thin layer of clay balm onto a teflon sheet. Roll out 20g (¾oz) silver clay to a thickness of five playing cards. Place the template onto the clay and cut around it with a clay pick or craft knife.

2 Take the excess silver clay and roll it out again to a thickness of five playing cards. Take the larger round cutter and cut a semi-circle shape into the top of the clay.

3 Take the medium-sized circle cutter and cut a semi-circle from the base of the clay. The clay shape should have a width of approximately 2cm (¾in).

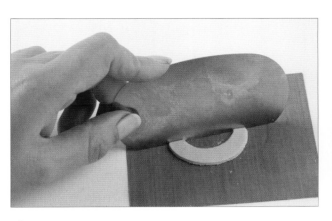

4 Trim the bottom edges of the semi-circle of clay with a tissue blade so that they are straight. This clay piece will form the body and wings of the swan. Allow the head and the body of the swan to dry completely.

5 After the pieces have dried, sand and smooth them all over with sponge sanding pads to remove any imperfections. Pay particular attention to the edges of each piece. Carefully sand these so that they are very smooth and slightly rounded.

6 Apply a generous amount of silver syringe clay to the base of the swan's neck on the back of the piece.

7 Stick the swan's neck to the body piece. Use a wet paintbrush to smooth away any excess clay and seal the join between both pieces.

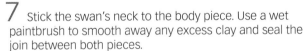

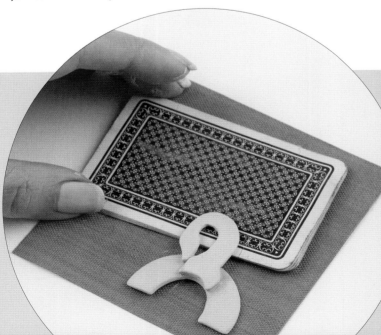

8 Place the piece on a teflon sheet with a pile of playing cards supporting the top of the neck. Allow the syringed clay to dry completely.

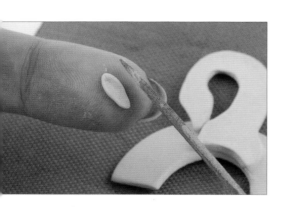
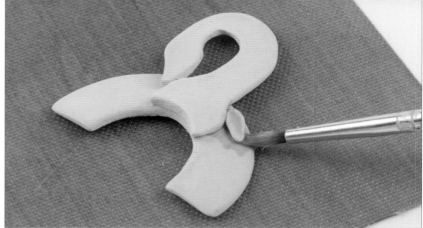

9 To form a feather, pinch off a small piece of the excess silver clay. Roll it into a short sausage shape, measuring approximately 5mm (¼in), and flatten it with a round needle file.

10 Apply some silver syringe clay to the back of the feather shape. Place it at the top of the swan's body next to the neck. Use a wet paintbrush to remove any excess syringe clay and seal the join between the two pieces.

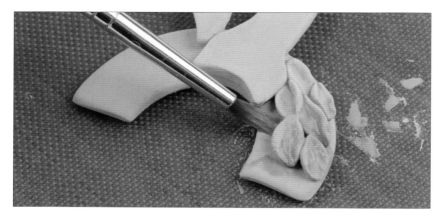

11 Repeat steps 9 and 10 to cover both sides of the swan's body with feathers, creating the wings. I have added about ten small feathers to each side of the body.

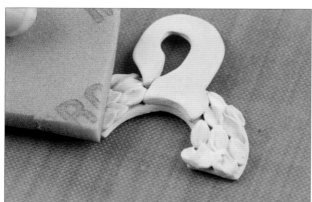
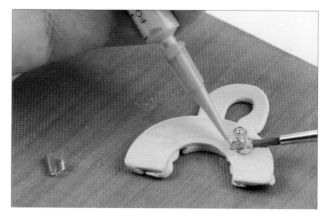

12 Allow the feathers to dry completely. Smooth any rough areas with a sponge sanding pad and polishing papers. Smooth the surface of the swan's neck and face with dry polishing papers.

13 Turn the swan over and apply a generous amount of syringe clay to the centre of the right-hand side of the body. Embed one part of the brooch setting into the syringe clay. Smooth the clay over the brooch setting with a wet paintbrush and remove any excess clay.

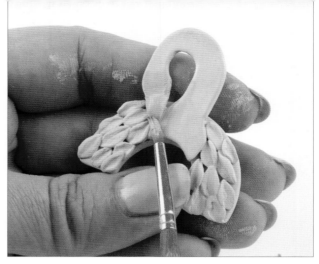

14 Repeat step 13 on the left-hand side of the swan's body to attach the second part of the brooch setting. Allow the settings to dry completely.

15 Pinch off a small piece of excess silver clay. Wet the clay and wet the end of the swan's beak. Press the clay onto the swan's beak to create a more three-dimensional appearance. Smooth the clay with a wet paintbrush. Use some syringe clay to place a dot of clay for the swan's eye.

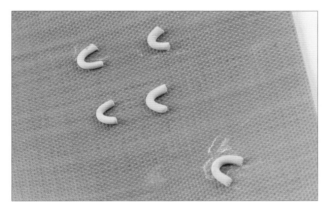

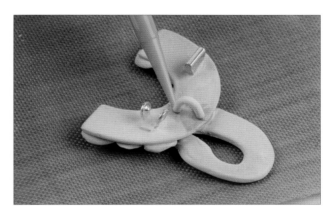

16 Roll some of the excess silver clay into a long, thin rope. Place the rope of clay on a teflon sheet. Cut the rope of clay into five pieces with a tissue blade, each one should measure approximately 1cm (½in) long. Use a wet paintbrush to gently form each of the pieces of clay into a 'c' shape. Allow these shapes to dry thoroughly.

17 Gently smooth away any excess clay or rough areas from the C-shaped pieces of dry clay with a dry paintbrush and a damp baby wipe. Use some syringe clay to attach one of the 'c' shapes to the back of the swan's body, in the centre at the top. Carefully smooth away any excess clay with a small, wet paintbrush.

18 Follow the process in step 17 to attach the other four 'c' shapes to the back of the swan's body. Spread the shapes out evenly across the body. Be careful to allow a space for the brooch pin to sit under the 'c' shapes.

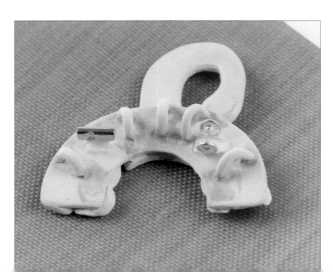

Key Technique: adding gold leaf

Adding gold leaf to metal is an ancient art known as *keum-boo*. The technique originated in Korea and consists of heating the metal to a temperature of 260–370°C (500–700°F), which increases the movement of its atoms. When pressure is added it causes an electron exchange at the surface between the two metals, creating a permanent bond between them. When you intend to add gold leaf to a piece, do not quench it in water straight after firing. Quenching opens up the pores in the silver. If the metal is porous, the gold can disappear into the tiny holes within the piece. It is easier to add gold leaf to fine silver because it is less porous than sterling silver. Before attaching the gold leaf to the silver, heat the silver using a gas torch, gas hob or a kiln. I find it easier to heat the piece with a gas torch because I can attach the gold leaf immediately without having to transfer the piece to another surface.

19 Allow the swan to dry completely before giving the piece a final sand and smooth all over with sponge sanding pads and dry polishing papers. Fire the swan according to the instructions on page 169. After firing, allow it to cool down naturally. Brush with a brass wire brush to reveal the silver.

20 Cut a piece of gold leaf the size and shape of the swan's beak. Heat the swan's beak with a gas torch on top of a fire brick. Heat the silver to the point where it is glowing a pale salmon-pink colour, then allow it to cool for five seconds.

top tip

Be careful not to overheat the metal – this can make the gold melt into the silver and disappear completely from the surface. Applying gold leaf takes a bit of practice so it is best to do it slowly. You may wish to practise first by applying a small scrap of gold leaf to a piece of fired silver. Look at the gold under a magnifying glass to check that it has evenly bonded to the surface of the silver.

21 Using a pair of fine tweezers place the piece of gold leaf on top of the beak and press down.

22 Hold the swan's neck with the tweezers and burnish the gold into place with a metal burnishing tool. Keep applying pressure with the burnishing tool until the gold has fused smoothly all over the beak. If there are any rough areas where the gold has not bonded with the silver, gently heat the piece again and continue burnishing the gold.

23 Allow the swan to cool before handling. Use an agate burnisher to polish the edges of the body, neck and feathers.

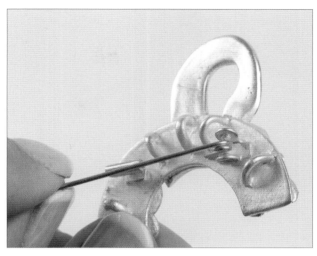

24 Place the end of the brooch pin inside the pin clasp.

25 Pinch the clasp together with the pair of chain-nose pliers to secure it in place.

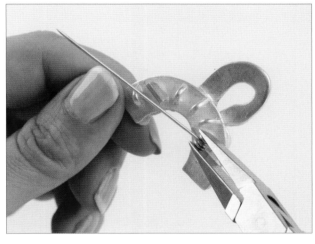

26 Place the brooch pin under the fastening then trim the brooch pin wire to the correct length with a pair of wire cutters.

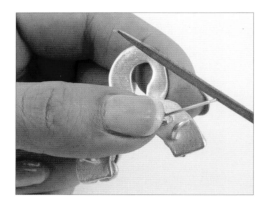

27 File the end of the brooch pin wire to sharpen it again so that it passes easily through clothing.

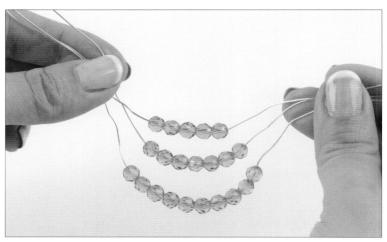

28 Take ½m (20in) of silver wire and cut it into three equal lengths. Thread five of the glass beads onto the first piece of wire, seven beads onto the second wire and ten beads onto the third wire.

30 Trim the excess wire with wire cutters.

29 Attach each of the wires to the back of the swan in ascending order. Thread the wires through the loops and wrap the wires around them to secure them in place. Be careful to ensure that the brooch pin can easily open and close after attaching the wires.

31 Arrange the beads so that they align well and form a smooth rounded shape that follows the curve of the wings. Your brooch is now ready to wear.

Tropical bird earrings

The wonderful thing about design is that you can pick and choose your inspiration. I've always been mesmerised by tropical birds and I decided to create my own tropical bird design that is a bit of a hybrid. It has the colourful beak and body shape of a toucan and the fabulous feathers and tail of a bird of paradise. What I like most about these pieces is the unusual use of colour. Using coloured pencils on the piece after firing gives the silver a beautiful contrast and vibrancy.

MATERIALS

Template (page 174), scissors and card

Clay balm

Teflon sheet

40g (1½oz) silver clay

Mini roller

Playing cards

Texture sheet

Clay pick or craft knife

Sponge sanding pads

Silver syringe clay

Small paintbrush

Cup of water

Pin vice

Polishing papers

Firing equipment

Wire brush

White gesso primer

Coloured pencils

Cocktail stick

Clear UV gel and UV lamp

Pearlescent paint, purple

10cm (4in) silver wire, 0.8mm gauge

Two blue glass faceted beads, 6mm (¼in)

Round-nose pliers

Chain-nose pliers

Eight silver jump rings, 6mm (¼in)

Two silver fish hook earring wires

Wire cutters

top tip

For the main body of the bird I chose a texture that looked like fish scales. This worked very well in the design because when it was turned into a bird shape the texture gave the impression of feathers.

1 Draw the bird shapes onto a piece of card and cut them out (see page 174). Apply a thin layer of clay balm to a teflon sheet and roll out 10g (⅓oz) silver clay to a thickness of five playing cards. Place a texture on top of the clay and press down firmly enough to leave a good impression in the clay but so that you avoid squashing the clay too thinly.

2 Place the template for the bird's body on top. Cut around it with a clay pick or craft knife. Repeat this process for the body of the second bird. Roll out another 10g (⅓oz) silver clay to a thickness of five playing cards, without texturing it. Place the template for the bird's neck onto the clay and cut around it. Repeat to create a neck for the second bird.

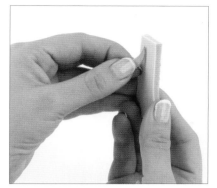
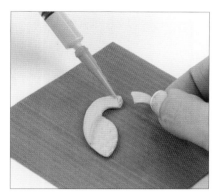

3 Allow the pieces to dry, then sand and smooth them. Be extra careful when sanding the neck pieces. They will be quite fragile because they are long and slim. Apply a generous layer of syringe clay to the back of one of the bird's necks and attach it to the left-hand side of one of the body shapes. Repeat the process with the second bird, attaching the neck on the right-hand side, and allow the pieces to dry.

4 Roll out the excess silver clay to a thickness of four playing cards. Place the beak template on top of the clay and cut around it with a clay pick. Repeat this process with the second beak. Allow the beaks to dry out fully and then sand and smooth them.

5 Apply some syringe clay to the end of the bird's face and attach the beak to this. Allow the piece to dry.

6 Apply a little more syringe clay to the join between the head and the beak and smooth the syringe clay with a wet paintbrush to seal any gaps between the two pieces. Repeat for the second bird. Leave to dry.

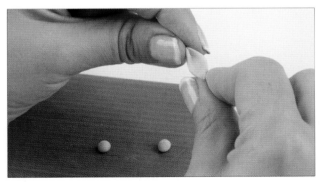

7 To create the tail, pinch off some of the excess silver clay and form it into a leaf shape measuring approximately 12mm (½in) long. Pinch the pointed ends of the clay together to make it more three-dimensional.

8 Pinch off two more pieces of clay and form these into leaf shapes that are a third smaller than the piece you created in step 7. Stick the three clay shapes together with syringe clay, placing the largest piece in the middle.

9 Repeat steps 7 and 8 to create the second tail. Allow the tail pieces to dry completely. Sand and smooth the birds and drill a hole at the base of each bird's body with a pin vice.

10 Roll out a thin rope of silver clay. Cut the rope into four pieces each measuring approximately 1cm (½in) long. Form one of the ropes into a loop shape and attach this to the top back of the tail with some syringe clay. Smooth the join with a wet paintbrush. Repeat this process on the back of the second bird's tail.

11 Form the other two pieces of clay into 'c' shapes and attach one to the back of each bird's head. This creates a bail for the jump ring to go through when the birds have been fired. Allow them to dry out completely.

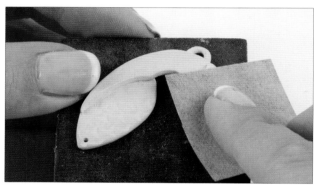

12 After drying, sand and smooth the birds all over with dry polishing papers.

13 Place the birds and their tails on some fibre blanket to support them during firing. Fire the pieces according to the instructions on pages 168–169.

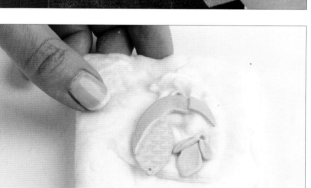

14 After firing, either allow the pieces to cool down or quench them in cold water. Brush the pieces all over to reveal the silver.

Key Technique: using coloured pencils and UV gel

15 Apply a thin layer of white gesso primer to the body and beak of each bird with a fine paintbrush.

16 Apply some white gesso primer to the centre of each of the tail feathers. Allow the gesso to dry, then apply a second coat to each of the pieces in the same areas.

17 After the second coat of gesso has dried, colour the pieces with coloured pencils. Colour the beak with orange and yellow. On the body, apply the colours in diagonal stripes using vibrant red, turquoise, yellow and orange.

18 Use green and yellow on the tail feathers. Use good-quality coloured pencils. The better quality the pencil, the more vibrant the colours will appear on the birds.

19 Pour some clear UV gel onto the areas where you have applied the coloured pencils. Use the end of a cocktail stick to spread the gel evenly across the coloured area and all the way to the edges of the pieces.

20 Place the pieces onto a piece of perspex and place the perspex under a UV lamp. The gel can take between five and thirty minutes to cure. Follow the manufacturer's instructions for curing the gel.

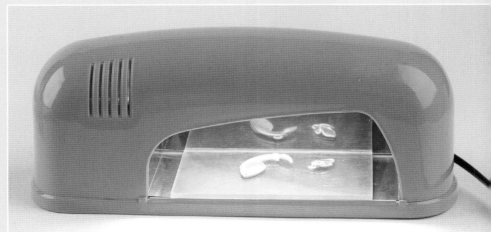

21 Add a dot of pearlescent paint to each of the bird's faces to create the eyes. Allow the paint to dry for three or four hours.

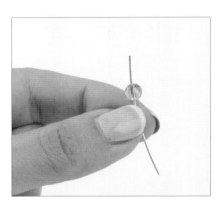

22 Use wire cutters to cut a 5cm (2in) length of silver wire. Thread a blue glass bead onto the wire.

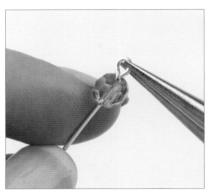

23 Create a loop in the end of the wire using round-nose pliers (see page 38).

24 Bend the other end of the wire at the other end of the bead to a 90-degree angle. Trim the wire so that there is 1cm (½in) remaining. Bend the wire to form a loop.

25 Use chain-nose pliers to open a jump ring and place it through the hole at the base of the bird's body. Close the jump ring. Open the loop at one end of the blue bead and attach this to the jump ring. Close the loop with the chain-nose pliers.

26 Take another jump ring and open it with the chain-nose pliers. Use this jump ring to connect the bird's tail and the wire loop at the base of the blue bead. Close the jump ring to secure it. Attach two further jump rings to the loop at the top of the bird's head. Attach an earring wire to the top jump ring. Repeat the process for the second earring.

Other colour techniques: colourising with alcohol inks

Alcohol inks are a perfect way of adding colour to fired metal clay pieces. The colours are very intense so a little goes a very long way. Alcohol inks come in a very wide range of colours, so you can experiment to your heart's content with these. They stain the metal but on large smooth areas the colour can rub off over time. The best results come from adding alcohol inks to deep textures, as I have done here to create this cloisonné effect.

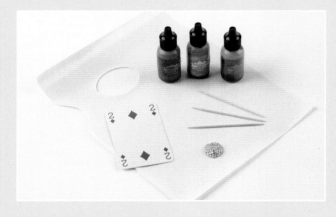

1 Place the alcohol ink bottles on a protective surface such as waxed paper. They stain everything they touch so always close the lids tightly and be very careful not to spill them on your furniture or work surfaces.

2 Place the fired metal clay piece on top of a playing card. Squeeze a drop of alcohol ink onto the playing card. Dip the end of a cocktail stick into the alcohol ink, then transfer it into the deep areas of texture.

3 Add a second drop of alcohol ink in a different colour. Apply the alcohol ink to your piece using the end of the cocktail stick.

4 Continue adding colour in the desired way. Squeeze out just one drop of alcohol ink at a time as the inks evaporate very quickly. When you are happy with the overall look, allow the ink to dry for a couple of hours. You can protect the ink from fading by applying a layer of protective varnish or Renaissance wax.

Other colour techniques:
using glass or enamel paints

Glass paints are another option for adding colour and interest to your metal clay pieces after firing. The glass paints come in a wide variety of different shades and often need to be baked in the oven to set them. Check the manufacturer's instructions for guidance. Enamel paints have interesting effects within them and dry at room temperature. Both of these colour options are quite robust and will withstand wear and tear without fading or peeling off the metal.

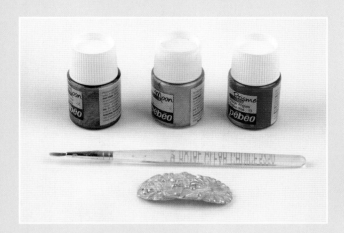

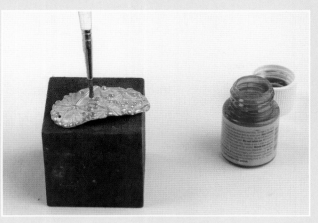

1 You will need to apply the paints using a very fine paintbrush. Ideally, add colour to a piece that has an interesting surface texture so you can pick out areas of colour. The texture of the piece shown here stands out in relief so is ideal for colouring.

2 Place the fired metal clay piece on top of a rubber block. Apply the first paint colour to the desired areas.

3 Clean your brush, then use it to apply the second colour. Repeat this process with the third colour.

4 Check the manufacturer's instructions for setting the paint. Glass paints usually need to be baked in the oven. The temperature required is quite a gentle heat so will not adversely affect the metal clay. If you are using enamel paints, allow the piece to dry overnight before wearing.

Beneath the Ocean Waves

In this ocean-themed section of this book I have combined interesting techniques within designs that are inspired by my favourite marine life. These designs are inventive and fun and I find their richness of colour and texture really appealing.

Techniques covered:

Octopus pendant

This is quite a large piece, so the design lends itself perfectly to using copper clay, which is much less expensive than silver clay. The satin finish and the colour of the fired copper is almost luminous and helps the details on the tentacles stand out well. Sculpting and moulding all the tentacles is a little fiddly, but it is well worth it because the overall effect is very fluid.

MATERIALS

50g (1¾oz) copper clay
Ceramic tile
Tissue blade
Cup of water
Paintbrush
Teflon sheet
Sponge sanding pad
Polishing papers
Firing equipment
Pickling equipment
Pearlescent paint, white and purple
Four gold-coloured jump rings, 8mm (5/16in)
Chain-nose pliers
60cm (24in) length of gold-coloured chain

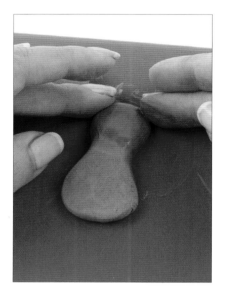

1 Take 50g (1¾oz) of copper clay. Cut off 10g (1/3oz) of it and set this aside. Roll the large piece of copper clay into an oval shape. Place it onto a ceramic tile and begin to flatten the top of the clay to form the octopus's head. Pull the bottom of the clay downwards to form the tentacles.

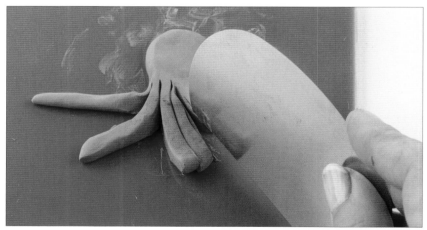

2 Use a tissue blade to cut the lower part of the clay into five equally sized 'tentacles'.

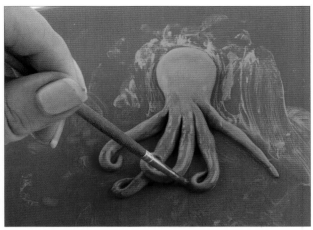

3 Wet your fingers and begin to mould and shape each of the tentacles. Getting the tentacles to the right width and length can take a little time, so do this gently and carefully until you achieve the desired tapering effect.

4 Use a wet paintbrush to move the tentacles around and position them how you want. Use the paintbrush to help curl up the ends of the tentacles.

5 Roll out the other 10g (¹/₃oz) of copper clay into three separate ropes that are a similar length and thickness to the other tentacles. Attach these new tentacles to the octopus, sealing the clay pieces to the back. Shape the ends of the tentacles you have added with the wet paintbrush. You will need to ensure that two of the tentacles are curving upwards – form a loop with the clay at the ends to create bails for the chain.

6 Allow the octopus to dry out completely. This a large piece of clay and you will have added lots of water to it during the shaping process. You will need to allow longer than usual for the piece to dry out. When the octopus is completely dry, sand and smooth it with a sponge sanding pad and dry polishing papers. Be extra careful when sanding around the tentacles as these will be very fragile.

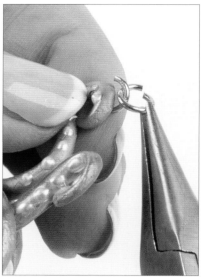

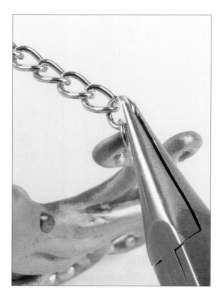

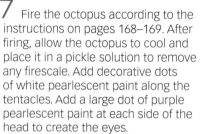

7 Fire the octopus according to the instructions on pages 168–169. After firing, allow the octopus to cool and place it in a pickle solution to remove any firescale. Add decorative dots of white pearlescent paint along the tentacles. Add a large dot of purple pearlescent paint at each side of the head to create the eyes.

8 Open a jump ring with chain-nose pliers and feed it through one of the tentacle loops on the right-hand side. If you suspect that it will be difficult to feed a second jump ring through the first once it is closed around the tentacle, open up a second jump ring and insert it before closing the first.

9 Attach one end of the chain to the open jump ring and close the jump ring with the pliers.

10 Repeat the process in steps 8 and 9 of attaching the jump rings and the other end of the chain to the top tentacle on the left-hand side of the octopus. Your pendant is now complete and ready to wear.

Fish earrings

Creating a pair of tropical fish earrings gave me the opportunity to add some sparkle, by setting crystals in epoxy clay. The beauty of this technique is that any crystals can be set into the special two-part resin clay, so you don't need to worry about their suitability for firing.

MATERIALS

30g (1oz) silver clay

Clay balm

Teflon sheet

Mini roller

Playing cards

Oval shape template

Clay pick

Tissue blade

Sponge sanding pads

Snake roller

Ceramic tile

Silver syringe clay

Small paintbrush

Cup of water

Polishing papers

Firing equipment

Brass wire brush

Burnishing tool

Silver polish

Epoxy clay for crystals kit, gold

Assorted crystal chatons, in the colours and sizes of your choice

Two pairs of chain-nose pliers

Four silver jump rings, 6mm (¼in)

Two silver fish hook earring wires

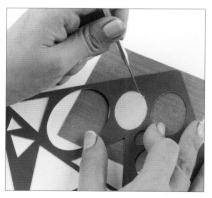

1 Roll out 10g (⅓oz) of silver clay to a thickness of five playing cards.

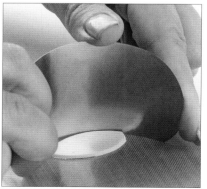

2 Place an oval shape template measuring approximately 4cm (1½in) long on top of the clay. Cut around the inside of the oval shape with a clay pick.

3 Take a tissue blade and bend the blade so that it is curved. Trim the edges of the clay oval to form a fish shape. Repeat these steps to create the second fish shape. Set both of these pieces of clay aside to dry out thoroughly. After the fish shapes have dried, sand them with sponge sanding pads to remove any imperfections.

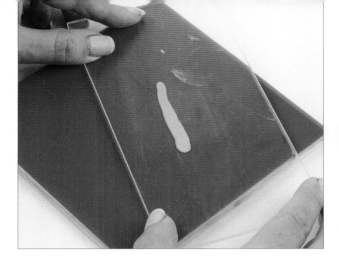

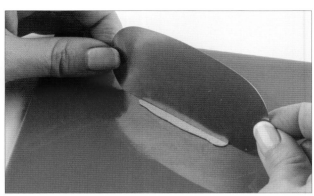

4 Take the excess silver clay and place it on a ceramic tile. Roll the clay into a rope with a snake roller, to a length of approximately 5cm (2in). Flatten the rope of clay by pressing down firmly onto it with the snake roller.

5 Trim the edges and the ends of the strip of clay with a tissue blade. Repeat to create a second strip of clay the same width and length as the first one.

6 Apply a line of syringe clay along the edges of one of the dried clay fish shapes. Place one of the strips of clay along the edge of the fish so that the excess clay at the end of the strip follows the curve along to form the fish's tail. Place the second strip of clay along the opposite edge of the fish shape. Use a wet paintbrush to remove any excess clay and to seal the join between the clay pieces.

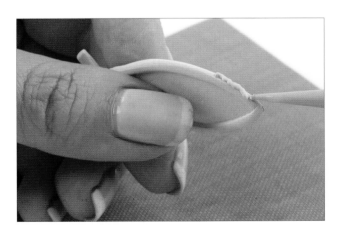

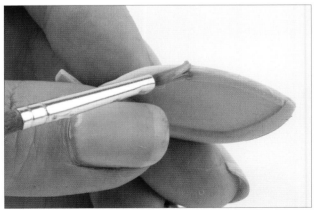

7 Allow the piece to dry thoroughly, then sand the piece. Apply some more syringe clay to the edges of the fish.

8 Smooth the syringe clay with a damp paintbrush to create a smooth and seamless join between the pieces of clay. Repeat these steps to create the second fish earring.

9 Take some of the excess silver clay and roll it into two thin ropes of clay, each one measuring approximately 2.5cm (1in). Wet the ropes of clay with a small paintbrush and form them both into loop shapes.

10 Allow the loops to completely dry. Attach one to the top underside of each fish, using some syringe clay. Smooth the clay and join the pieces together using a wet paintbrush.

11 Allow both pieces to dry completely. After drying, sand and smooth both earrings with sponge sanding pads and dry polishing papers. Take particular care when sanding the ends of the fish tail and the loop at the top of the fish. These areas will be very fragile.

12 Fire both fish earrings according to the instructions on pages 168–169.

top tip

When firing a pair of earrings, try to fire both at the same time. Shrinkage of the silver clay can vary according to the temperature used, the time you fire the pieces for and the firing method used. If you do need to fire the pieces separately, make careful note of the temperature the first piece was fired at and exactly how long you fired it for. Ensure that you follow the same process and use the same firing method for the second earring.

13 Allow the pieces to cool or quench them in cold water. Brush the pieces with a brass wire brush to reveal the silver. Polish the pieces with a burnishing tool and silver polish.

Key Technique: using epoxy clay and crystals

14 Put on the protective gloves from the epoxy clay kit. Take equal quantities of each of the two parts of the clay. Mix these together until the clay is one even colour with no streaks in it.

15 Push the epoxy clay into the centre of each silver fish earring. Smooth the clay so that it is evenly distributed across the fish and remove any excess.

16 Take the wooden gem-setting stick from the kit and manipulate the wax on the end to make it sticky. Pick up one of the crystal chatons by placing the sticky end of the gem-setting stick on the top of the crystal. Push the pointed end of the chaton into the clay. Push down firmly until you have placed the chaton at the desired depth. Ensure that the top of the chaton is level with the clay.

top tip

The epoxy clay is very sticky so it is important to wear latex gloves to protect your hands. However, it can be difficult to keep the surface of the clay smooth when you are applying it with gloves. Before adding the crystal chatons, rub a wet baby wipe across the surface of the clay. This gives it a beautifully smooth and even surface.

17 Continue to add the chatons to the epoxy clay in the desired pattern. Add two slightly larger, dark coloured chatons at the top end of the fish to give the effect of eyes. Repeat the process to complete the second earring. Allow the clay to cure according to the manufacturer's instructions.

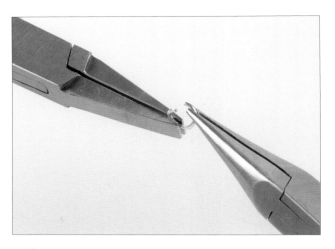

18 Take one of the jump rings and open it with two pairs of pliers, by moving one pair of pliers towards you and one pair of pliers away from you. Attach the jump ring to the loop at the top of the fish, then close it.

19 Open a second jump ring and attach this to the first jump ring. Close the jump ring.

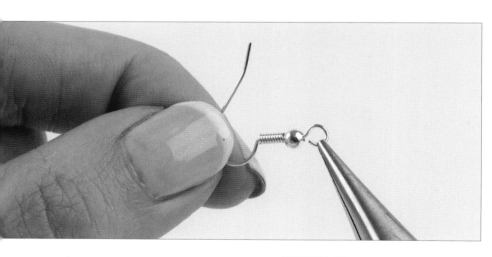

20 Open the loop at the base of a fish hook earring wire with a pair of pliers.

21 Attach the open loop of the fish hook earring wire to the second jump ring. Close the loop in the earring wire with pliers. Repeat these steps to complete your second fish earring.

Starfish ring

I wanted to create my own take on the beautiful design of the starfish. The starfish shape on this ring curves upwards, and the texture inside it is taken directly from something found beneath the ocean waves: a sea urchin shell. The half-drilled pearl set inside the starfish and the golden-bronze colour accents give this ring an added touch of glamour.

MATERIALS

Wooden ring mandrel
Ring-sizing papers
Ring-measuring gauge
20g (¾oz) silver clay
Teflon sheet
Clay balm
Playing cards
Mini roller
Tissue blade
Clay pick
Small paintbrush
Cup of water
Sponge sanding pad
Silver syringe clay
Two-part silicone moulding putty
Small sea urchin shell
Snake roller
Template (page 174), card and scissors

Curved object such as a door handle or a small lightbulb
Pin vice
Rubber block
2.5cm (1in) fine silver wire, 0.8mm gauge
Chain-nose pliers
Wire cutters
Polishing papers
Firing equipment
Wire ring brush
Enamel paint, bronze
Bronze-coloured half-drilled pearl, 6mm (¼in)
Resin glue

Key Technique: ring-making the traditional way

This is how to make a ring from scratch. Before you begin, measure your ring finger carefully: metal clays shrink during firing, so if you are creating a ring from silver clay, you must make the ring between two and four sizes bigger (depending on the width of the ring shank). Make the ring two sizes bigger if you are using copper or bronze.

1 Measure your finger using a ring-measuring gauge. If you want your ring to have a very slim shank (approximately 5mm/¼in wide), create the clay ring two sizes bigger. For a medium shank (approximately 1cm/½in wide) make it three sizes bigger. For a wide ring shank (1.5cm/²⁄₃in or more wide), the ring should be four sizes bigger.

2 Take a ring-sizing paper and cut off the excess paper at the cut mark (this is the sticky end of the paper). Wrap the ring-sizing paper around a ring mandrel at the point along the mandrel that is the size of the ring (allowing for shrinkage). Adjust the paper until the sticky edge meets the correct measurement line. Stick the edge of the paper down firmly.

3 Apply some clay balm to a teflon sheet. Take 10g (⅓oz) silver clay and roll this into a strip that is long enough to encircle the ring mandrel with an overlap of about 2cm (¾in). The clay should be the thickness of five playing cards. Trim the edges of the strip of clay with a tissue blade.

4 Wrap the clay around the ring paper on the mandrel so that the ends of the clay overlap. Aim for the centre of the black line on the paper.

5 Cut through the centre of the overlap in the clay with a tissue blade. Hold the blade at an angle of about 45-degrees. This will create a closer joint when you join the two ends together. Remove the excess clay and press the two ends together gently to form a join in the clay.

6 Use a clay pick or other sharp instrument to bind the two pieces of clay together. Make light dovetail-style incisions to pull the two pieces of clay together. This method creates a smoother join on the ring.

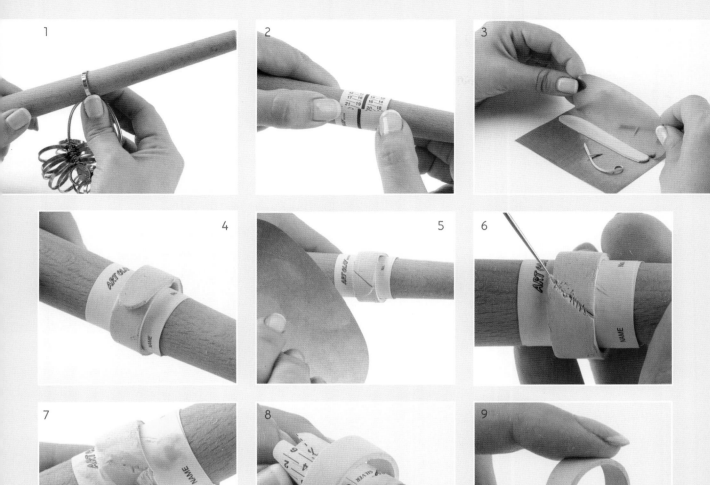

7   Smooth the join with a small wet paintbrush. Allow the ring to dry on the mandrel. If you are drying the ring in a warm place, allow it dry for one hour. If you are leaving the ring to dry at room temperature, allow it to dry for 24 hours.

8   After the ring has dried, slip it off the mandrel by gently twisting the ring sizing paper. Carefully insert a clay pick or needle tool between the paper and the clay ring and push the paper inwards to remove it.

9   Smooth the rough areas around the edge, inside and outside the ring with a sponge sanding pad. Add some syringe clay to fill the join inside and out. Smooth the join using your finger or a damp paintbrush. Allow the ring to dry again, repeat the process until you have a perfect finish and so that the join on the inside of the ring can no longer be seen.

top tip

If you are adding a top to your ring (as we will here with the starfish) you do not need to worry about getting a perfect finish along the join on the outside of the ring, as it will be covered. However, it is essential that you create a seamless join on the inside of the ring. This is so that the ring is strong and the join cannot be seen or felt when the ring is being worn.

Key Technique: making moulds

Mould making is an excellent way of capturing a perfect replica of an object or texture. I prefer to use a silcone-based, two-part moulding putty. These types of moulds are strong but flexible and can be stored and used time and again. The silicone allows you to release the clay effortlessly from the mould without needing to add a release agent such as clay balm or olive oil.

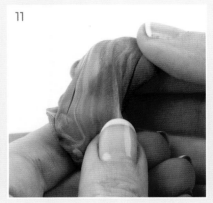

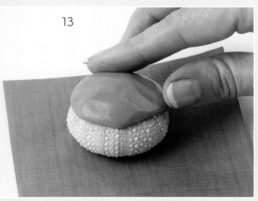

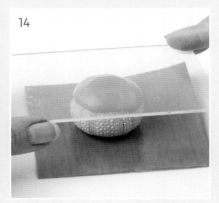

10 Two-part silicone moulding putty is supplied in two separate containers marked A and B. It is essential that you take equal quantities of each part to create your mould.

11 Mix the two parts together as quickly as you can before the putty begins to 'cure' or set.

12 When the two parts are thoroughly mixed together, the putty will have an even colour with no streaks or marbling.

13 Press the putty over the surface of a sea urchin shell to create the mould. Distribute the putty onto the shell so that it is an even thickness all the way across.

14 Push a flat object, such as a snake roller, down on top of the moulding putty to create a flat base for the mould.

15 Allow the putty to cure according to the manufacturer's instructions. Press your nail into the edge of the mould to check that it has fully cured. If your nail leaves in indent in the mould then the putty has not yet cured. Once the mould has cured, gently flex it to release it from the shell. Be gentle with it to ensure that you do not tear the mould.

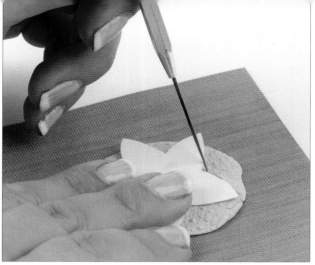

16 Trace the starfish (see page 174) onto a piece of card and cut it out to create a template. Take 10g (¹/₃oz) of silver clay and mix this with any of the excess clay from the ring you made earlier. Press the clay into the mould. Make sure that the clay is wide enough to fit the starfish template.

17 Gently peel the wet clay away from the sea urchin mould. Apply a thin layer of clay balm to a teflon sheet and lay down the clay with the sea urchin texture facing upwards. Lightly place the starfish template on top of the clay and cut around the shape with a clay pick.

18 To create the curved effect, place the starfish textured-side down onto a curved object such as a door handle or a small light bulb. Apply a thin layer of clay balm to the object before adding the clay. Press the clay down gently so that it assumes the curved shape and allow the clay to dry fully.

19 When the clay has dried, sand the edges and back of the starfish with a sponge sanding pad. Do not sand the front, because this will wear away the texture.

20 To decorate the starfish, apply little dots of clay with the syringe. Work out from the centre of the starfish along each of the points.

21 Allow the clay dots to dry completely. Sand each of the dots gently with a sponge sanding pad to remove the peak of each dot created by the syringe and to leave each dot looking and feeling smooth.

22 Place the starfish on a rubber block or craft mat and drill a hole through the centre with a pin vice.

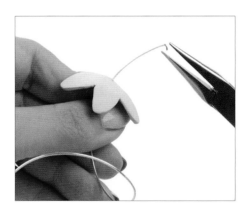

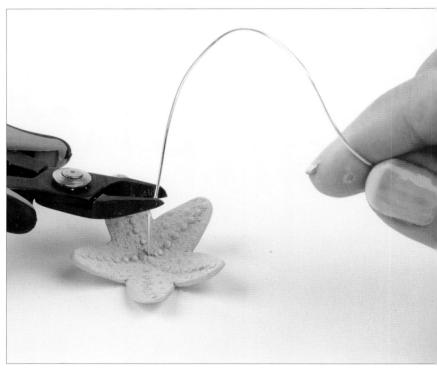

23 Thread a piece of fine silver wire through the hole in the centre of the starfish. Bend the end of the wire to a 90-degree angle to form an 'L' shape.

24 Pull the wire upward so that the 'L' shape of wire is flush with the base of the starfish. Trim the other end of the wire with wire cutters, leaving approximately 2.5cm (1in) of wire protruding from the centre of the starfish.

25 Polish the inside and outside of the silver clay ring with dry polishing papers, so that the ring is as smooth as possible.

26 Apply a generous amount of silver syringe clay to the base of the starfish to cover the wire and to secure it to the ring shank.

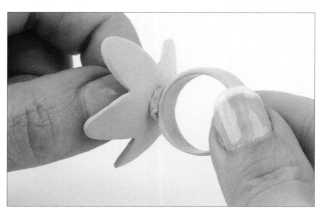

27 Attach the starfish to the ring shank. Ensure that you position the starfish so that it sits directly over the join in the ring.

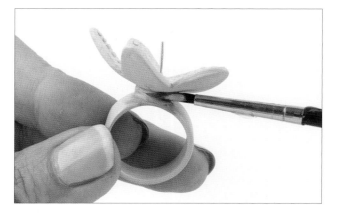

28 Use a wet paintbrush to remove the excess syringe clay and to smooth the join between the two pieces. Allow the ring to dry. After drying, do any final sanding necessary to refine the ring before firing.

29 Fire the ring according to the instructions on pages 168–169. After firing, quench the ring in cold water to cool it, or allow the ring to cool down naturally. Brush the ring to reveal the silver. You may find it easier to push the wire to one side as you brush the centre of the starfish.

30 Wet a piece of green polishing paper and wrap it around the handle of a paintbrush or pen. Use this to polish the inside of the ring. Polish the ring by working your way down through the different gradients of wet polishing papers, beginning with the roughest one.

31 Use a small paintbrush to apply a light coating of bronze enamel paint to each of the silver dots on the inside of the starfish. Allow the paint to dry according to the manufacturer's instructions.

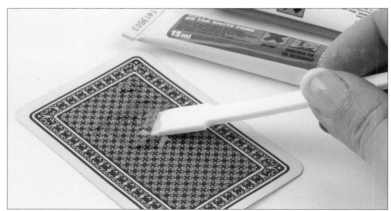

32 Trim the wire in the centre of the starfish so that it is long enough to fit inside the pearl, so that the pearl sits flush on top of the starfish. Mix the resin glue on a card according to the manufacturer's instructions.

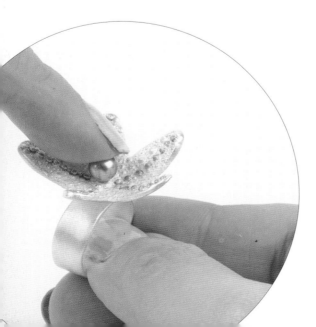

33 Apply some glue to the wire in the centre of the starfish. Place the pearl onto the wire and press it down. Remove any excess glue with a damp baby wipe. Support the ring while the glue is drying so that the pearl is pointing upward. Allow the glue to dry for 24 hours before wearing your ring.

Other Beautiful Creatures

In this section I have included designs for some of Mother Nature's other beautiful creatures, along with some creatures of myth and legend that we all know and love. These projects combine many of the techniques covered earlier in the book. I hope the application of these techniques within the different designs will give you some added inspiration.

Techniques covered:

• Making silver beads 149

Butterfly pendant

I could not have a section devoted to beautiful creatures without creating a butterfly. I think what makes them so attractive is their delicate beauty and what they represent symbolically: transformation. Butterflies live on average for just two weeks, but by capturing their elegance in a piece of jewellery, you can ensure that your silver clay butterfly lives forever.

MATERIALS

Teflon sheet
Clay balm
Mini roller
Playing cards
20g (¾oz) silver clay
Circle-shaped cutter –
   3cm (1¼in) diameter
Paintbrush
Cup of water
Sponge sanding pad
Polishing papers
Rubber block
Pin vice with diamond burr

Silver syringe clay
Cocktail stick
Fifteen–twenty clear cubic
   zirconia, 2mm (¹/₁₆in)
4cm (1½in) fine silver wire
Wire cutters
Polishing papers
Cotton bud
Pure alcohol
Firing equipment
Brass wire brush
Epoxy clay for crystals kit, gold
Crystal chatons in assorted
   bright colours, 3mm (¹/₈in)

Resin glue
Faceted glass crystal beads,
   4mm (³/₁₆in) – four petrol
   blue, two red, two green, one
   turquoise
Silver polish and a soft cloth
Burnishing tool
Two silver jump rings
Short lengths of silver chain,
   about 15cm (6in) in total
Chain-nose pliers
Seven silver head pins
Round-nose pliers
Silver necklace chain (the
   length of your choice)

1 Apply a light coating of clay balm to a teflon sheet. Roll out 20g (¾oz) of silver clay to a thickness of five playing cards. Cut out a circle shape with a cutter. Remove the excess clay from around the circle.

2 To create the butterfly's wings, use the circle cutter to cut away the left-hand side of the clay circle. This leaves a half-moon shaped piece of clay. Repeat to create the second wing. Allow the wings to dry.

3 To make the butterfly's body, take the remaining silver clay and roll it into a patty shape. Pinch the sides to mould it into an oval. Press the end of a paintbrush handle into the centre of the clay to create a hollow.

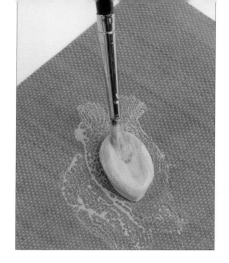

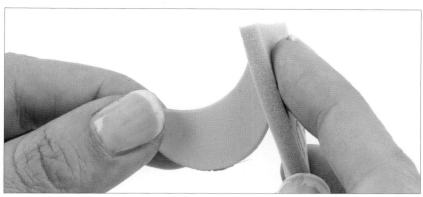

4 Pinch the ends of the clay shape to make them more pointed. Run a wet paintbrush over the surface of the clay to smooth the whole shape. Allow the body to dry fully.

5 Sand both of the wings and the butterfly's body all over with a sponge sanding pad and polishing papers.

6 Place one of the wings on top of a rubber block and drill seven or eight holes with a diamond burr, in a random arrangement. The burr holes should be deep enough for the cubic zirconia to sit within so that the tops align with the surface of the clay. Repeat for the second wing.

7 Add a small dot of silver syringe clay to the centre of each of the holes you have drilled.

8 Dip the end of a cocktail stick into some clay balm. Use this to pick up the flat top of a cubic zirconia and place it into one of the holes in the clay. Use the edge of the cocktail stick to push the cubic zirconia down firmly into the setting. Repeat steps 7–8 for the second wing.

9 Allow the wings to dry. Apply a generous amount of silver syringe clay to the back of the body and attach the wings to it with the cubic zirconia facing up against the body.

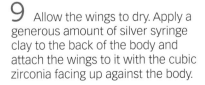

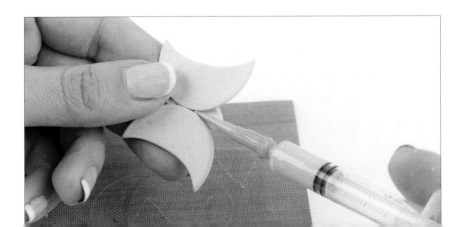

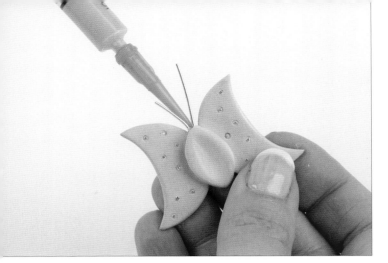

10 Apply a generous amount of syringe clay to the space at the back of the body between the wings. Cut two lengths of fine silver wire for the antennae, one slightly longer than the other. Push the wires into the syringe clay at the back of the head.

11 Smooth away any excess clay with a damp paintbrush and allow the piece to dry fully. Smooth the piece again with polishing papers. Do this very gently to avoid scratching the cubic zirconia.

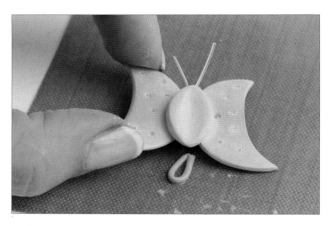

12 Roll two thin snakes of clay, each one measuring 1.5cm (²/₃in) long, and form them into loop shapes. Allow the loops to dry and gently sand them after drying. These will form the bails at the top and bottom of the butterfly.

13 Attach the bails to the back of the butterfly with syringe clay. Smooth away any excess clay with a damp paintbrush. Allow the clay to dry completely.

14 Sand the back of the piece to remove any imperfections. Fire the butterfly according to the instructions on pages 168–169.

top tip

Dip a cotton bud into some pure alcohol to clean away any clay from the cubic zirconia before firing.

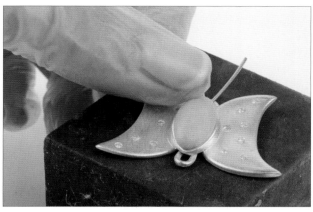

15 After firing, allow the butterfly to cool naturally or quench it in cold water. Brush the butterfly with a brass wire brush to reveal the silver.

16 Mix the epoxy clay and press it into the body of the butterfly. See page 127 for more detailed instructions about how to work with epoxy clay most effectively.

17 Set the crystal chatons into the clay with the gem-setting tool in the kit. Place the crystals in a random pattern, mixing up the colours to give the body a more interesting and colourful look.

18 Allow the epoxy clay to cure. Mix some resin glue and apply some glue to the very tip of each wire antennae. Place one of the petrol blue glass beads onto the end of each wire. Allow the glue to dry for 24 hours.

19 Add some silver polish to the piece and buff it with a soft cloth.

143

20 Clean the cubic zirconia once more with some pure alcohol to make them sparkle.

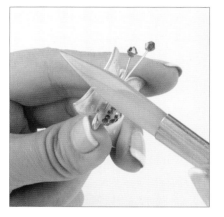

21 Burnish the edges of the piece with a burnishing tool to bring the metal to a high shine. This makes the piece sparkle a little more as it moves when it is being worn.

22 Open a jump ring with pliers and attach it to the loop at the base of the butterfly. Cut fives piece of chain to varying lengths ranging from 2.5 to 4cm (1 to 1½in). Attach the pieces of chain to the jump ring and close it with the pliers.

23 Thread one of the glass crystal beads onto a head pin. Thread the head pin wire onto the last link in one of the pieces of chain. Create a wrapped loop with the excess wire and the round-nose pliers. Trim off any excess wire. Repeat this process to attach the other glass beads to the chain ends. Attach the remaining beads at intervals along the chains.

24 Attach a jump ring to the centre link in the necklace chain. Attach the jump ring to the loop at the top of the butterfly. Close the jump ring with the pliers. Your necklace is now complete.

Snail bracelet

The humble snail isn't often chosen as a muse when it comes to jewellery design. I am fascinated with their simple shape and I wanted to give them a chance to become more glamorous by immortalising them in silver. I'm sure you haven't seen many snails with pearls at the end of their antennae... but you have now!

MATERIALS

Ceramic tile
20g (¾oz) silver clay
Snake roller
Teflon sheet
Cup of water
Small paintbrush
Sponge sanding pad
Polishing papers
Silver syringe clay
7.5cm (3in) fine silver wire, 0.8mm gauge
Wire cutters
Chain-nose pliers
Rubber block
Pin vice
Craft knife or tissue blade
Gas torch
Firing brick
Tweezers
Firing equipment
Brass wire brush
Agate burnisher
Resin glue
One light grey half-drilled pearl, 8mm (⁵⁄₁₆in)
Two light grey half-drilled pearls, 6mm (¼in)
20cm (8in) sterling silver wire
Soft leather bracelet

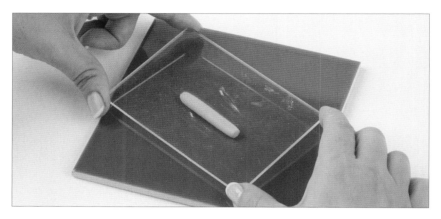

1 Place 10g (¹⁄₃oz) of silver clay onto a ceramic tile. Roll it into a sausage shape with your fingers. Use a snake roller to roll the clay into a rope shape measuring approximately 10cm (4in) long.

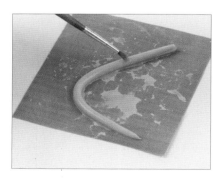

2 Place the rope of clay onto a piece of teflon. Use a paintbrush to wet it. Allow the water to soak into the clay for a minute. This makes the clay more supple and easier to form into the snail's shell.

3 Use the paintbrush to move the rope of clay around to form it into a tight spiral shape. Allow the clay to dry out thoroughly. Depending upon how much additional water you have added, you will need to allow the clay to dry out for longer than normal.

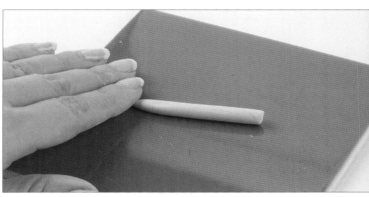

4 When the clay has fully dried out, sand and smooth the piece all over using a sponge sanding pad and dry polishing papers.

5 Take the other 10g ($^1\!/_3$oz) of silver clay and roll it into a sausage shape on top of your ceramic tile.

6 Roll the clay with your fingers to form a length of clay that is quite bulbous at the top and that tapers to a point at the end. The clay should measure approximately 5cm (2in) long. Wet the clay to keep it supple and malleable.

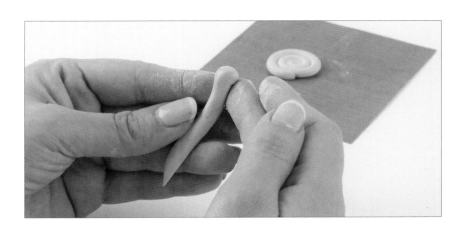

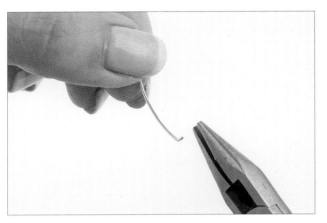

7 Apply some silver syringe clay along the bottom edge of the dried snail's shell. Place the length of wet clay along the bottom of the snail shell and stick the two pieces together. Allow the snail to dry completely.

8 Cut two pieces of fine silver wire measuring approximately 1.5cm ($^2\!/_3$in) each. Bend one end of each piece of wire to form an 'L' shape.

9 Push the wires into the wet clay at the top of the snail's head, inserting the 'L' shape. Push one of the wires in slightly further than the other so that one wire protrudes slightly higher than the other.

10 Allow the snail to dry out completely. After drying, add some syringe clay to the area where the wires meet the clay and fill any gaps between them. Smooth the syringe clay with a wet paintbrush.

11 Apply some syringe clay to the join between the snail's shell and its body. Use the wet paintbrush to smooth away any excess clay and to fill any gaps between the two pieces. Allow the snail to dry again.

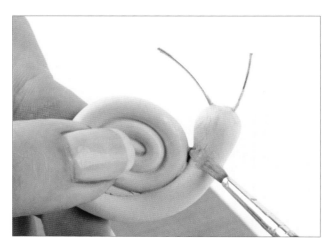

12 Place the snail on top of a rubber block or craft mat and drill a hole through the centre of the shell with a pin vice.

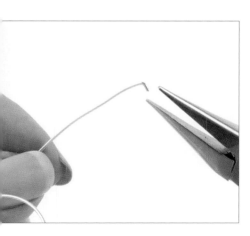

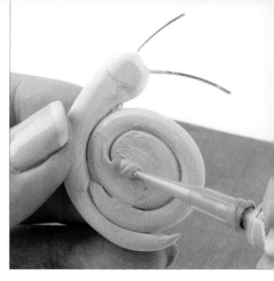

13 Take another length of fine silver wire and bend the end of it with a pair of pliers to form an 'L' shape.

14 Trim the wire to a length of approximately 2.5cm (1in) and thread the end of the wire up through the hole in the centre of the snail shell at the back. Pull the wire through so that the 'L'-shaped end of it sits flush with the back of the shell.

15 Apply some syringe clay to the wire at the back of the piece. Use a damp paintbrush to smooth the clay and give a smooth coverage of the wire. Allow the piece to dry.

Key Technique: making silver beads

Sometimes you will be left with small pieces of lump or syringe clay. You may have even left a piece of clay to dry out by mistake and the piece is so small it is not worth grinding up to turn back into lump clay. A good use for this leftover clay is to dry it out and convert it into silver beads.

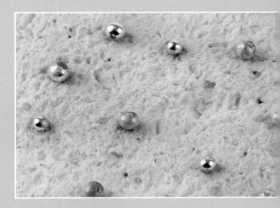

16 Use a craft knife or tissue blade to chop up dried clay into tiny pieces.

17 Place the pieces on top of a firing brick. Heat them with a gas torch. You need to heat them much more strongly than you would normal silver clay pieces. On this occasion, the objective is to melt the silver. When the silver begins to melt it glows orange and begins to shimmer.

18 Slowly, as each piece melts, it rolls itself into a perfectly round silver ball. Tiny pieces will melt quickly and form their ball shape instantly. Larger pieces will require longer and more concentrated heating from the gas torch. Allow the silver balls to cool or quench them in water before use.

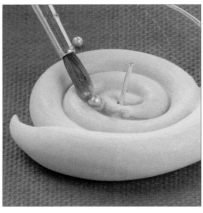

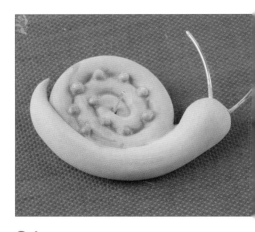

19 Add a dot of syringe clay to the places on the snail shell where you would like to apply the silver balls. Carefully place each one of the silver balls in position on the shell with a pair of tweezers.

20 Use a paintbrush to apply a watered down paste solution over each silver ball and onto the clay around it.

21 Continue to set all of the silver balls in position. Wetting the balls and the surrounding clay with the thin paste solution allows the balls to sinter more effectively with the silver clay piece during firing.

22 Allow the piece to dry fully. Sand and smooth the piece with dry polishing papers. Be very gentle as you do this to avoid dislodging the silver balls.

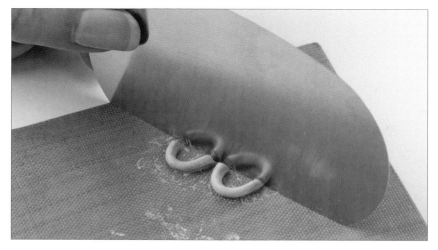

23 Take a small piece of silver clay and roll it into a rope of clay measuring 2.5cm (1in) long. Cut the rope of clay into two equal pieces with a tissue blade. Form the pieces into 'c' shapes and trim their ends with a tissue blade to neaten. Allow the pieces to dry out completely.

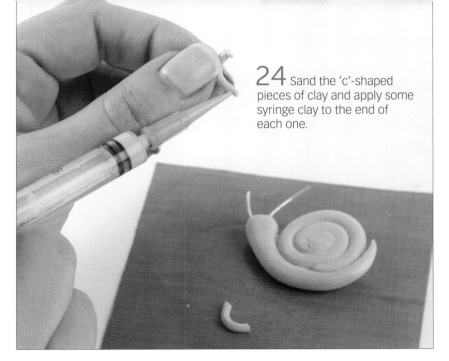

24 Sand the 'c'-shaped pieces of clay and apply some syringe clay to the end of each one.

25 Attach each 'c' shape to the back of the snail. These will form the bails that will allow you to connect the snail to the leather bracelet. Smooth the areas around the bails with a damp paintbrush, to remove any excess clay and seal the join between the pieces of clay.

26 Allow the snail to dry fully. Do any final sanding and smoothing of the back and front of the piece. Place the snail on some fibre blanket to support it during firing. Fire the snail according to the instructions on pages 168–169.

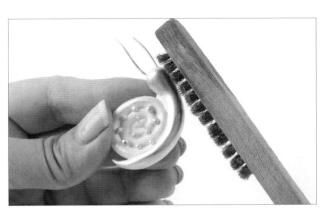

27 After firing, allow the piece to cool or quench it in cold water. Brush the piece with a wire brush to reveal the silver. Gently bend the wires to one side to make it easier to brush the snail all over.

28 Polish the edges of the snail shell and the snail's body with an agate burnisher.

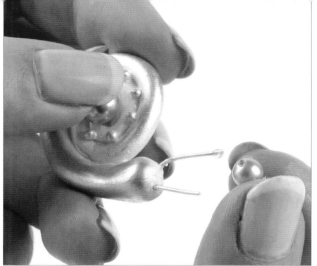

29 Trim the wire in the centre of the shell with wire cutters to the length that allows the large pearl to sit flush with the shell. Mix some resin glue according to the manufacturer's instructions.

30 Apply the glue to the wire in the centre of the shell and place the large pearl onto the wire. Apply some resin glue to the ends of both wires on the top of the snail's head. Attach a smaller pearl to the end of each wire. Allow the glue to dry for 24 hours before wearing.

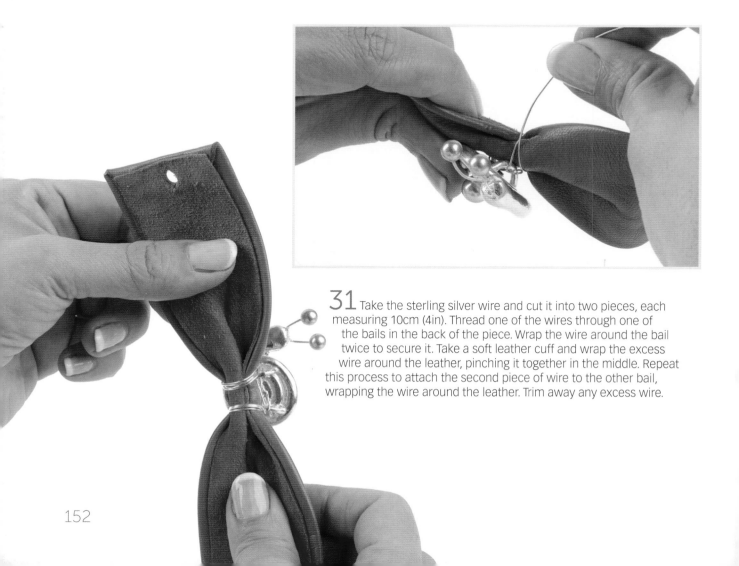

31 Take the sterling silver wire and cut it into two pieces, each measuring 10cm (4in). Thread one of the wires through one of the bails in the back of the piece. Wrap the wire around the bail twice to secure it. Take a soft leather cuff and wrap the excess wire around the leather, pinching it together in the middle. Repeat this process to attach the second piece of wire to the other bail, wrapping the wire around the leather. Trim away any excess wire.

Unicorn pendant

Unicorns always remind me of the fairytales from my childhood. These mythical creatures are beautiful to look at and so very magical. I wanted the horn to be three-dimensional and I thought long and hard about how I would create this. Looking around my studio for inspiration, I found a pile of shells I collected during a beach holiday in Wales. The long spiral-shaped shell was the perfect horn for my unicorn. I added a gold leaf accent to the horn after firing, to give my silver unicorn an extra special touch of magic.

MATERIALS

Template (page 174), card, pencil and scissors
Clay balm
Teflon sheet
40g (1½oz) silver clay
Mini roller
Playing cards
Clay pick or craft knife
Needle file
Long spiral shell
Two-part silicone moulding putty
Slim paintbrush
Sponge sanding pad
Polishing papers
Snake roller
Ceramic tile
Cup of water
Silver syringe clay
Pencil
Rubber block or craft mat

Pin vice
Tissue blade
Drinking straw
Firing equipment
Wire brush
Burnishing tool
Gas torch
Gold leaf
Tweezers
Fire brick
Gold-coloured necklace chain (the length of your choice)
Five gold-coloured jump rings, 6mm (¼in)
Round-nose pliers
Chain-nose pliers
Wire cutters
1m (40in) gold-coloured chain
Ten small aluminium beads in assorted metallic colours, 4mm (³/₁₆in)
Ten gold-coloured head pins, 5cm (2in)

1 Draw the unicorn shape onto a piece of card and cut this out to create a template (see page 174).

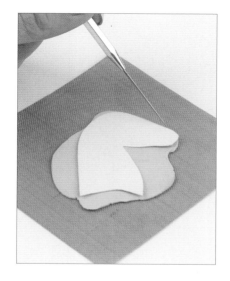

2 Apply a thin layer of clay balm to a teflon sheet. Roll out 30g (1oz) of silver clay to a thickness of five playing cards. Place the unicorn template on top of the clay and cut around the shape with a clay pick or craft knife.

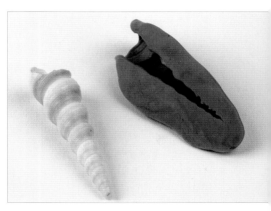

3 Remove the excess clay. Press the rounded end of a needle file (or similar tool) into the clay at the end of the nose to create the impression of the unicorn's nostril.

4 Apply a thin layer of clay balm to a playing card. Bend the card along the centre to form a curved shape. Place your clay onto the playing card and leave this to dry until the unicorn has dried in a curved shape. Remove the clay from the playing card and allow it dry completely.

5 Take a mould of the long spiral-shaped shell with silicone moulding putty. Mix the putty and create the mould by following the instructions on pages 132–133.

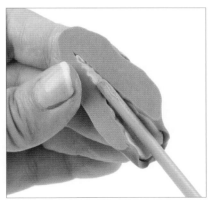

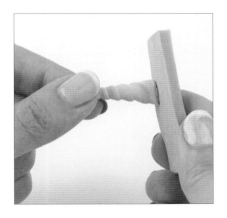

6 Take some of the excess silver clay and press this firmly into the shell mould.

7 Use the end of a slim paintbrush to hollow out the centre of the shell shape and to push the clay firmly into the mould so that it makes a very clear impression. Remove any excess clay and allow the clay to dry inside the mould.

8 If you are drying the clay in a warm place, gently remove it from the mould after an hour. If you are drying it at room temperature, allow 24 hours. The clay may still be damp inside, so allow it to dry out completely. After drying, refine any rough edges with a sponge sanding pad.

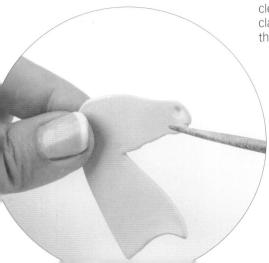

9 After the unicorn's head has dried, sand the whole piece with a sponge sanding pad. Refine the areas in between the neck and the head with a needle file. Smooth the back and front of the piece with dry polishing papers.

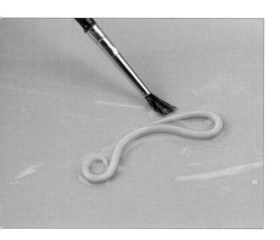

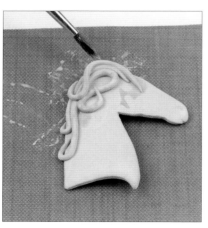

10 Roll a long, thin rope of clay on a ceramic tile with a snake roller. Wet the rope of clay thoroughly with a small paintbrush.

11 Use the paintbrush to lift up the rope of clay and transfer it onto the head of the unicorn. Move the clay rope around to form the fringe at one end of the rope and the curls of the unicorn's mane at the other end.

12 Repeat this process, creating further ropes of clay, until you have created a full mane and a fringe for the unicorn. Allow the unicorn to dry out completely.

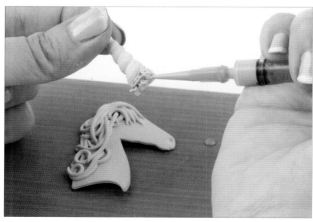

13 Carefully sand and smooth the mane of the unicorn with dry polishing papers.

14 Apply a generous amount of silver syringe clay to the base of the unicorn's horn at the front.

15 Stick the horn to the back of the unicorn's head exactly in the centre point between the top of the head and nose. Angle the horn so that it is tilting slightly forward. Use a wet paintbrush to smooth away any excess syringe clay and to seal the join between the two pieces.

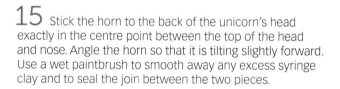

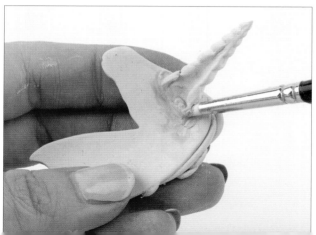

16 Allow the piece to dry completely. Place the unicorn face down on a rubber block or craft mat and drill five holes at the base of the neck. Mark out the holes with a pencil before drilling. Ensure that the holes are equally spaced and at least 5mm (¼in) from the edges of the clay.

17 Roll out a strip of silver clay to a thickness of four playing cards. The strip of clay should measure approximately 2cm (¾in) long and 5mm (¼in) wide. Flex a tissue blade so that it is curved and trim the edges of the strip of clay to form an elongated ellipse shape.

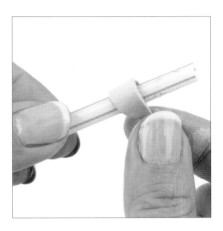

18 Wrap the strip of clay around a drinking straw to form a bail. Apply some syringe clay to the inside edge of one of the pointed ends of the strip. Pinch the ends to seal them together.

19 Apply some syringe clay to the base of the bail and place it onto the back of the unicorn's head, near the top. Gently smooth the edges of the clay bail onto the dry clay beneath to seal them together.

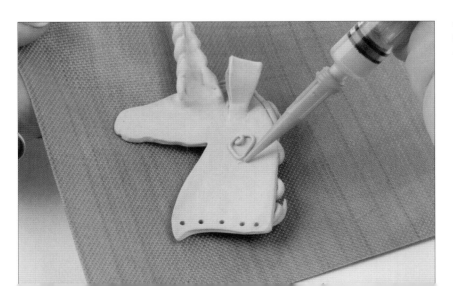

20 Allow the clay to dry fully. Sand and smooth the back of the piece with a sponge sanding pad and dry polishing papers. If you want, you could add a 'maker's mark' with syringe clay. I like to add a small heart to the back of my pieces, as this is my logo. Add whatever shape you wish, or perhaps your initials.

21 After the syringe clay has dried, the piece is ready to fire. Support the unicorn with fibre blanket so that it does not slump during firing. Fire the piece in a kiln according to the instructions on pages 168–169.

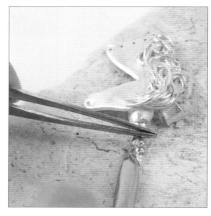

22 After firing, allow the unicorn to cool at room temperature. You will be adding gold leaf to the horn so do not quench it in cold water, as this makes the silver more porous. Brush the piece with a wire brush.

23 Use a burnishing tool to polish the edges of the unicorn and its mane to bring them to a high shine.

24 Heat the unicorn's horn with a gas torch and apply the gold leaf using a metal burnisher. You can find more detailed instructions about how to do this on page 106.

25 Allow the piece to cool down naturally – do not quench it in cold water. Thread the gold-coloured necklace chain through the bail. Cut different lengths of gold-coloured chain and attach these to jump rings through each of the five holes at the base of the unicorn's neck.

26 Thread an aluminium bead onto a head pin. Attach the head pin to the base of one of the lengths of chain with a wrapped loop. Repeat this process and attach a bead to the end of each piece of chain. Attach another bead to a link in the middle of each length of chain to complete.

Dragon pendant

Of all of the creatures from myth and legend there is none more powerful than the dragon. I researched lots of different dragon shapes and the one that I found most appealing was the Chinese river dragon. This one doesn't have wings and looks more like a serpent, but is just as fiery and fearsome as all the other dragons. In Chinese culture, dragons are the symbol of strength, power and good luck. I wanted my dragon to be golden, so bronze clay was perfect for this. It is also the ideal clay to carve into at the dry-clay stage.

MATERIALS

40g (1½oz) bronze clay
Snake roller
Ceramic tile
Cup of water
Clay modelling tool
Rubber block
Sponge sanding pad
Needle file
Pin vice
Carving tool
Polishing papers
Firing equipment
Pickling equipment
Brass wire brush
Metal burnishing tool
7.5cm (3in) gold-
    coloured wire
Leather pendant
Awl
7.5cm (3in) bronze-
    coloured wire
Necklace of your choice
    (I used a string of beads)

1 Roll out the bronze clay onto a ceramic tile using a snake roller. Roll the clay to a length of approximately 12cm (5in). As you roll, apply slightly more pressure on one side, so one end is thinner and the other more bulbous. Use your fingers to taper the thinner end so that it gradually ends in a point.

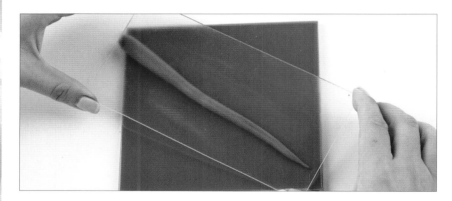

2 Wet the clay with your fingers and allow the clay to soak up the water for thirty seconds. Gently shape the clay to form the undulating curves of the dragon. Curl the tail of the dragon so that it forms a loop at the end.

3 Use a clay modelling tool to make an incision into the bottom part of the dragon's head. Remove a small 'v'-shaped piece of clay to create the dragon's open mouth.

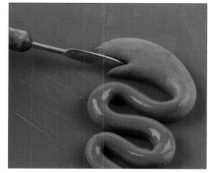

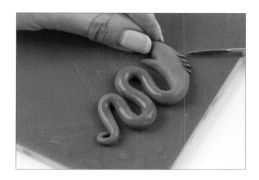

4 Use the modelling tool to make a series of incisions along the back of the dragon's head to create its horns. Allow the dragon to dry out completely.

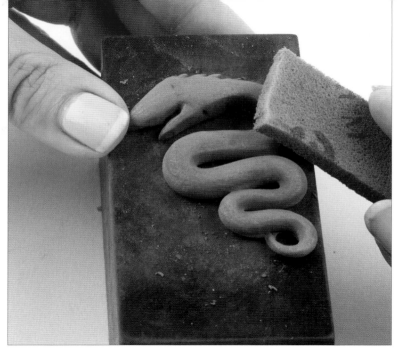

5 After the dragon has dried, sand it with a sponge sanding pad to ensure that the surface is very smooth and to remove any imperfections in the clay.

6 Use a needle file to refine the areas around the dragon's mouth and horns.

7 Use the pointed end of the needle file to carve the effect of the dragon's eye and to create ridges inside the mouth to give the impression of sharp teeth.

8 Carve the effect of scales all the way along the body with the sharp end of the needle file.

9 Drill a pair of holes near the edge of the first curve of the dragon's body with a pin vice. Drill a further two holes near the edge of the second curve. You will use these holes to attach the dragon to the leather pendant.

10 Use a carving tool to carve out tiny pieces of clay all along the body and tail to deepen the effect of the scales.

11 Give the piece a final smooth all over with dry polishing papers.

12 Fire the dragon according to the instructions on pages 168–169. Allow the dragon to cool after firing. Place in a pickle solution for between five and thirty minutes to remove any firescale. Remove the piece from the pickle solution and rinse in cold water.

13 Brush the piece to reveal the beautiful, golden-bronze colour. Polish the dragon with a metal burnishing tool. With an awl, make holes in the leather pendant to correspond with the holes in the dragon's body. Thread some gold-coloured wire through the holes in the front of the piece and attach it to the leather by twisting the ends. Trim off any excess wire. Make a hole at the top of the leather. Thread some bronze wire through the hole and create a wrapped loop for a bail. You can now attach the pendant to the necklace of your choice.

Bull pendant

Bull heads were once just the decorative domain of wild-west cowboys. With the rise in popularity of kitsch jewellery, the bull's head has been given a stylish new lease of life as an accessory that is very cool and fashionable. So here is my precious metal version of this iconic symbol. The golden tones of bronze fit this piece so well.

MATERIALS

50g (1¾oz) bronze clay
Teflon sheet
Cup of water
Small paintbrush
Ceramic tile
Snake roller
Tissue blade
Sponge sanding pad
Polishing papers
Clay modelling tool
Firing equipment
Pickling equipment
Brass wire brush
Metal polish and a soft cloth
2m (78¾in) gold-coloured chain
Gold-coloured necklace clasp
Two gold-coloured jump rings, 6mm (¼in)
Chain-nose pliers

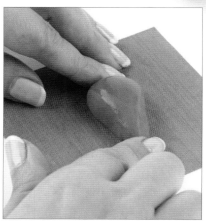

1 Place 40g (1½oz) of bronze clay on a teflon sheet and wet it with your fingers. Mould and shape the clay into an elongated triangle shape. Round the more pointed end of the shape to form the bull's nose.

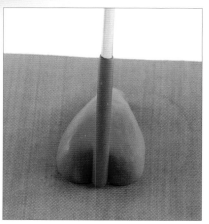

2 Push a slim, round-handled object such as a paintbrush or needle file handle into the clay at the top of the bull's head in the centre. This forms the dip in the top of the bull's head.

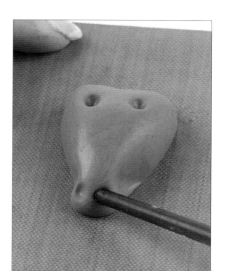

3 Push the end of a paintbrush into the clay to create the bull's eyes and the nostrils at the end of the nose. Allow the clay to dry completely.

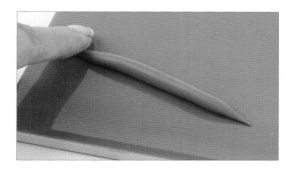

4 Roll out 10g (¹/₃oz) of bronze clay on a ceramic tile using a snake roller. Roll the clay into a rope shape measuring approximately 5cm (2in) long. Roll each end of the clay rope with your fingers to form a point.

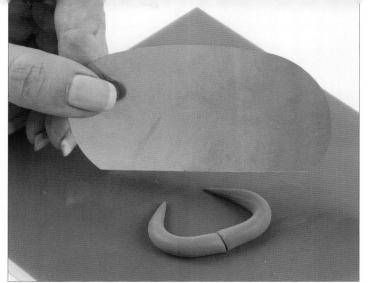

5 Wet the clay and allow the water to sink in for a minute. Curve the ends of the clay upwards to form the bull's horns. Cut the piece of clay in two with a tissue blade. Allow the pieces to dry fully.

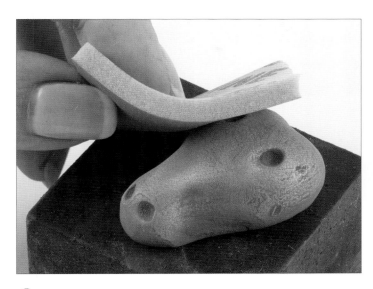

6 When the pieces have dried, sand each with a sponge sanding pad and dry polishing papers.

7 Take a small piece of bronze clay and use a clay modelling tool to mix it into a sticky paste with a little water.

8 Apply a generous amount of bronze paste to the flat end of one of the horns.

165

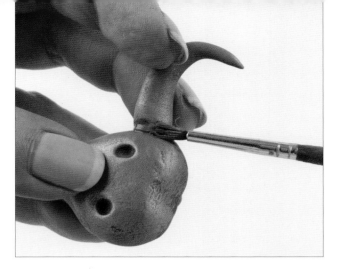

9 Attach the horn to one side of the bull's head. Hold the clay in place for a few minutes to allow the bronze paste to adhere to the dry clay. Repeat this process with the second horn. Allow the piece to dry. Add more paste if necessary to ensure the elements are well connected and secure.

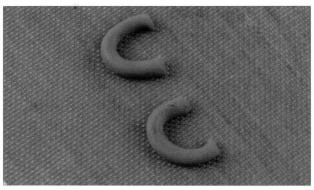

10 Roll out a rope of bronze clay to a length of approximately 2.5cm (1in). Cut the rope of clay in half and form each piece of clay into a 'c' shape. These will form the bails for the necklace. Allow the pieces to dry.

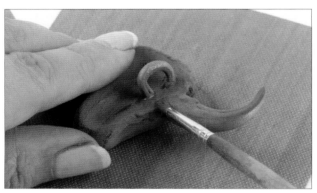

11 After the clay shapes have dried, sand them to remove any imperfections. Mix some more bronze paste and apply this to the ends of the 'c' shapes. Attach them to the back of the bull's head. Smooth the join between the pieces using a damp paintbrush. Allow to dry fully.

12 Do any necessary final sanding on the back of the piece. Fire the bull according to the instructions on pages 168–169. Allow the bull to cool down. Place the bull in a pickle solution for between five and fifteen minutes to remove any firescale. Rinse the piece in cold water and brush it with a brass wire brush to reveal the bronze colour.

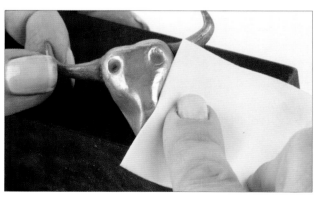

13 Polish the bull's face with wet polishing papers and metal polish to bring it to a high shine. Attach the gold chains and the necklace clasp to complete the piece: I ran a doubled length of gold-coloured chain through each of the bails on the back of the bull's head, and completed the piece with a matching gold-coloured clasp.

Firing times

Given below are the tried-and-tested firing times and temperatures for every project in the book. Kiln firing copper or bronze clay requires two stages – see the box to the right for further information.

Kiln firing

Stage 1: Open fire on wire mesh on a gas stove, or kiln fire at 350°C (662°F) in a metal box on top of coconut-activated carbon.

Stage 2: Fire in a metal box; cover piece(s) with a 5cm (2in) layer of coconut-activated carbon.

PROJECT	GAS STOVE	GAS TORCH	KILN
CAT PENDANT: COPPER pages 42–45	Cannot be fired using this method.	Cannot be fired using this method.	Stage 1: 10 minutes Stage 2: 900°C (1652°F) for 60 minutes
SAUSAGE DOG PENDANT: SILVER pages 46–49	Cannot be fired using this method	Cannot be fired using this method	650°C (1202°F) for 30 minutes or 750°C (1382°F) for 10 minutes or 800°C (1472°F) for 5 minutes
MOUSE CHARMS: SILVER, COPPER AND BRONZE pages 50–55	Copper and bronze cannot be fired using this method Silver: 10 minutes	Copper and bronze cannot be fired using this method Silver: 3 minutes	**Copper:** Stage 1: 10 minutes Stage 2: 900°C (1652°F) for 30 minutes **Bronze:** Stage 1: 10 minutes Stage 2: 820°C (1508°F) for 30 minutes **Silver:** 650°C (1202°F) for 30 minutes or 750°C (1382°F) for 10 minutes or 800°C (1472°F) for 5 minutes
SCOTTY DOG RING: COPPER pages 56–59	Cannot be fired using this method	Cannot be fired using this method	Stage 1: 10 minutes Stage 2: 900°C (1652°F) for 60 minutes
RABBIT PENDANT: SILVER pages 60–65	Cannot be fired using this method	Cannot be fired using this method	650°C (1202°F) for 30 minutes or 750°C (1382°F) for 10 minutes or 800°C (1472°F) for 5 minutes
SNAKE PENDANT: COPPER pages 68–71	Cannot be fired using this method	Cannot be fired using this method	Stage 1: 10 minutes Stage 2: 900°C (1652°F) for 60 minutes
SNAKE RING: COPPER pages 72–73	Cannot be fired using this method	Cannot be fired using this method	Stage 1: 10 minutes Stage 2: 900°C (1652°F) for 60 minutes
ELEPHANT PENDANT: COPPER AND SILVER pages 74–81	The copper cannot be fired using this method Silver: 10 minutes	The copper cannot be fired using this method Silver: 5 minutes	**Copper:** Stage 1: 10 minutes Stage 2: 900°C (1652°F) for 90 minutes **Silver:** 650°C (1202°F) for 30 minutes or 750°C (1382°F) for 10 minutes or 800°C (1472°F) for 5 minutes

PROJECT	GAS STOVE	GAS TORCH	KILN
LION BRACELET: SILVER AND BRONZE pages 84–89	Cannot be fired using this method	Cannot be fired using this method	**Bronze:** Stage 1: 10 minutes Stage 2: 820°C (1508°F) for 90 minutes **Silver:** 650°C (1202°F) for 30 minutes or 750°C (1382°F) for 10 minutes or 800°C (1472°F) for 5 minutes
SWALLOW RING: SILVER pages 94–101	Cannot be fired using this method	Cannot be fired using this method	650°C (1202°F) for 30 minutes or 750°C (1382°F) for 10 minutes or 800°C (1472°F) for 5 minutes
SWAN BROOCH: SILVER pages 102–109	Cannot be fired using this method	Cannot be fired using this method	650°C (1202°F) for 30 minutes or 750°C (1382°F) for 10 minutes or 800°C (1472°F) for 5 minutes
TROPICAL BIRD EARRINGS: SILVER pages 110–115	10 minutes	5 minutes	650°C (1202°F) for 30 minutes or 750°C (1382°F) for 10 minutes or 800°C (1472°F) for 5 minutes
OCTOPUS PENDANT: COPPER pages 120–123	Cannot be fired using this method	Cannot be fired using this method	Stage 1: 10 minutes Stage 2: 900°C (1652°F) for 120 minutes
FISH EARRINGS: SILVER pages 124–129	Cannot be fired using this method	Cannot be fired using this method	650°C (1202°F) for 30 minutes or 750°C (1382°F) for 10 minutes or 800°C (1472°F) for 5 minutes
STARFISH RING: SILVER pages 130–137	Cannot be fired using this method	Cannot be fired using this method	650°C (1202°F) for 30 minutes or 750°C (1382°F) for 10 minutes or 800°C (1472°F) for 5 minutes
BUTTERFLY PENDANT: SILVER pages 140–145	10 minutes	Cannot be fired using this method	Stage 1: 10 minutes Stage 2: 900°C (1652°F) for 60 minutes
SNAIL BRACELET: SILVER pages 146–153	Cannot be fired using this method	Cannot be fired using this method	650°C (1202°F) for 30 minutes or 750°C (1382°F) for 10 minutes or 800°C (1472°F) for 5 minutes
UNICORN PENDANT: SILVER pages 154–159	Cannot be fired using this method	Cannot be fired using this method	650°C (1202°F) for 30 minutes or 750°C (1382°F) for 10 minutes or 800°C (1472°F) for 5 minutes
DRAGON PENDANT: BRONZE pages 160–163	Cannot be fired using this method	Cannot be fired using this method	Stage 1: 10 minutes Stage 2: 820°C (1508°F) for 120 minutes
BULL PENDANT: BRONZE pages 164–167	Cannot be fired using this method	Cannot be fired using this method	Stage 1: 10 minutes Stage 2: 820°C (1508°F) for 180 minutes

Firing natural gemstones

Many tests have been done on gemstones and their capacity to endure heat. Research has shown that many gemstones at the highest end of the Moh's scale of hardness can survive firing. Many lab-grown cubic zirconia are also suitable to be set first, then fired in place (see page 172).

The table below shows the results of tests carried out by metal clay artisans Judi Weers and Kevin Whitmore of Rio Grande, a supplier of metal clay tools and resources in the USA. These charts are only a guide and results cannot be guaranteed. If there is a gemstone that you would like to use and it is not on this list, I would advise you to carry out your own research or testing before you fire it.

warning!

When firing copper and bronze clays with a gas torch it is critical that you quench your pieces in cold water immediately after firing. However, no gemstone would survive going from such intense heat to cold so quickly, so I recommend that if you are torch firing copper and bronze clay pieces, you should set the gemstones after firing (see page 78 for information on how to create a bezel).

NATURAL GEMSTONES	SURVIVED KILN FIRING AT 650°C (1202°F)	SURVIVED KILN FIRING AT 800°C (1472°F)	SURVIVED KILN FIRING AT 900°C (1652°F)	SURVIVED GAS TORCH (SILVER CLAY ONLY)
AMBER	No	No	No	No
ANDALUCITE	Yes	Yes	Yes	Not tested
APATITE	Yes	Turned white	Turned white	Not tested
BERYL (AQUAMARINE; EMERALD)	No	No	No	Not tested
BLACK SPINEL	Yes	Yes	Yes	Not tested
BLACK STAR SAPPHIRE	Yes	Not tested	Not tested	Not tested
BLUE SAPPHIRE	Yes	Yes	Turned a lighter colour	Yes
CHALCEDONY	No	No	No	No
CHRYSOBERYL (CATS EYE; ALEXANDRITE)	Yes	Yes	Yes	Not tested
DENIM LAPIS	Yes	Not tested	Not tested	Not tested
GREEN MOONSTONE	Yes	Yes	Turned a yellowish colour	Not tested
GREEN TOPAZ	Yes	Yes	Yes	Not tested

NATURAL GEMSTONES	SURVIVED KILN FIRING AT 650°C (1202°F)	SURVIVED KILN FIRING AT 800°C (1472°F)	SURVIVED KILN FIRING AT 900°C (1652°F)	SURVIVED GAS TORCH (SILVER CLAY ONLY)
GREEN TOURMALINE	Yes	Not tested	Not tested	Not tested
HAEMATITE	Yes	Not tested	Not tested	Not tested
IOLITE	Yes	Turned a darker colour	Turned a metallic colour	Not tested
LABRADORITE	Yes	Turned milky	Turned milky	No
MOONSTONE (IRID WHITE – TRANSLUCENT)	Yes	Yes	Yes	Not tested
OREGON SUNSTONE	Yes	Yes	Turned a lighter colour	Not tested
ORISSA GARNET	Yes	Turned a metallic colour	Turned a metallic colour	Not tested
PERIDOT	Yes	Turned a metallic colour	Turned a metallic colour	Yes
RAINBOW MOONSTONE	Yes	Yes	Turned an irid-blue colour	Not tested
RED GARNET	Yes	Turned a metallic colour	Turned a metallic colour	Not tested
RHODOLITE GARNET	Yes	Yes	Turned a metallic colour	Yes
RUBY	Not tested	Not tested	Not tested	Yes
STAR DIOPSIDE	Yes	Yes	Yes	Not tested
TANZANITE	Yes	Not tested	Not tested	Yes
TOPAZ (GREEN & WHITE)	Yes	Yes	Yes	Not tested
TOURMALINE	No	No	No	Not tested
WHITE TOPAZ	Yes	Yes	Yes	Not tested
ZIRCON	Yes	Yes	Yes	Not tested

Firing cubic zirconia

Cubic zirconia are gemstones grown in a laboratory and these survive particularly well when fired. Not all types of cubic zirconia retain their original colour so this list is well worth referring to if you want to ensure a specific colour within your design.

LABORATORY-GROWN GEMSTONES	SURVIVED KILN FIRING AT 650°C (1202°F)	SURVIVED KILN FIRING AT 800°C (1472°F)	SURVIVED KILN FIRING AT 900°C (1652°F)	SURVIVED GAS TORCH (SILVER CLAY ONLY)
BLACK: OPAQUE	Yes	Yes	Yes	Yes
CHAMPAGNE: TRANSPARENT	Yes	Yes	Yes	Yes
CLEAR: TRANSPARENT	Yes	Yes	Yes	Yes
DARK AQUA: TRANSPARENT	Turned a purple-blue colour	Turned a purple-blue colour	Turned a purple colour	Not tested
DARK BLUE: TRANSPARENT	Yes	Yes	Yes	Yes
DARK RED: TRANSPARENT	Yes	Yes	Yes	Yes
EMERALD GREEN: TRANSPARENT	Turned a brownish-red colour	Turned red	Turned red	Not tested
ORANGE: TRANSPARENT	Yes	Yes	Yes	Yes
PALE LAVENDER: TRANSPARENT	Yes	Yes	Yes	Yes
PURPLE: TRANSPARENT	Yes	Yes	Yes	Yes
RED: TRANSPARENT	Yes	Yes	Yes	Yes
TANZANITE: TRANSPARENT	Turned red	Turned dark red	Turned dark red	Not tested
YELLOW: TRANSPARENT	Yes	Yes	Yes	Yes

Glossary

Assay Office
A UK institution set up to test the purity of precious metals. The Assay Office stamps a hallmark onto items to certify their metallurgical content.

Awl
A long pointed tool for making holes in materials such as leather and wood.

Bail
A component used to attach a pendant to a necklace. The bail is normally placed where the necklace hangs.

Bezel
A rim that encompasses and fastens a jewel, stone or other object into a piece of jewellery.

Cabochon
A stone with a flat bottom with the sides rising up into a dome on the stone's top.

Crystal chaton
An imitation gem made of paste that has its pavilion backed with metal foil or silver to reflect light.

Findings
Components that connect pieces of jewellery together such as jump rings, head pins, earring wires and clasps.

Firescale
A reddish-brown crust that appears on copper and bronze pieces when they are fired and the metal comes into contact with oxygen.

Keum-boo
A Korean jewellery-making technique that involves bonding 24-carat gold leaf to another metal by heating the metal to 500°C (932°F).

Oxidisation
The action of oxygen on copper and bronze when the metals are heated. Oxidisation creates colour changes in the metals.

Pickle
Pickle is a solution used to remove oxidisation and other impurities from the surface of metals such as sterling silver, copper and bronze. A pickle is an acid bath and, in some ways, is similar to the brine used to pickle vegetables.

Sintering
The welding together of particles of metal by applying heat below the melting point.

Supplier

I would like to thank **Bead House**, which kindly supplied me with metal clays, gemstones, findings and jewellery making materials.
www.beadhouse.co.uk
telephone: 01484 485111

Templates

All the templates are given at actual size.

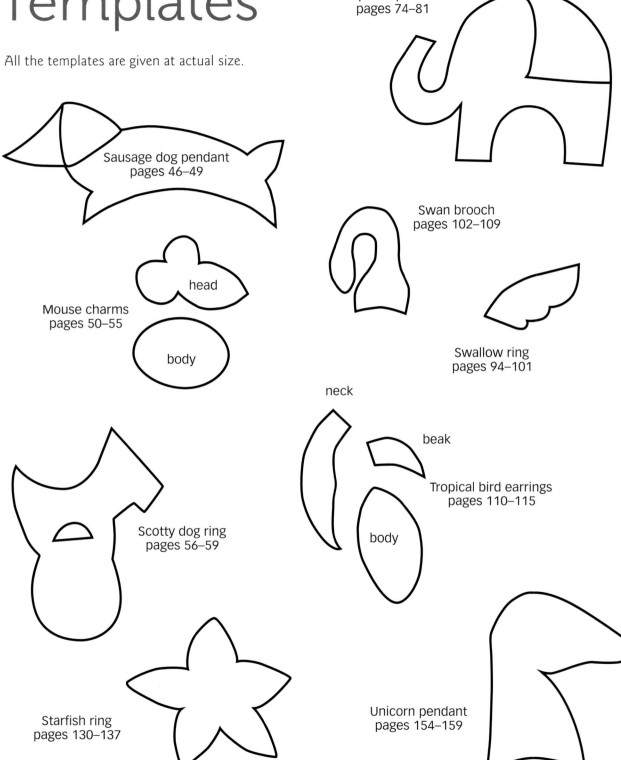

Elephant pendant
pages 74–81

Sausage dog pendant
pages 46–49

Swan brooch
pages 102–109

head

Mouse charms
pages 50–55

body

Swallow ring
pages 94–101

neck

beak

Tropical bird earrings
pages 110–115

Scotty dog ring
pages 56–59

body

Unicorn pendant
pages 154–159

Starfish ring
pages 130–137

Index